About the Author

Jane Rudden is an established writer in the field of literacy education. She holds an Ed.D. in curriculum and instruction with a concentration in reading. She is an author for Kendall/Hunt Publishing Group and Pearson Education Group, and a volunteer text reviewer for the Pennsylvania Breast Cancer Coalition (PBCC).

Jane lives and works in south central Pennsylvania. She writes near the sands of the Atlantic Ocean beaches on Fenwick Island, Delaware.

If We Must Dance, Then I Will Lead

A Memoir of Breast Cancer Survival

Jane Rudden

iUniverse, Inc.
New York   Bloomington

iUniverse books may be ordered through booksellers or by contacting:

iUniverse
1663 Liberty Drive
Bloomington, IN 47403
www.iuniverse.com
1-800-Authors (1-800-288-4677)

Because of the dynamic nature of the Internet, any Web addresses or links contained in this book may have changed since publication and may no longer be valid. The views expressed in this work are solely those of the author and do not necessarily reflect the views of the publisher, and the publisher hereby disclaims any responsibility for them.

ISBN: 978-1-4502-1178-9 (sc)
ISBN: 978-1-4502-1176-5 (hc)
ISBN: 978-1-4502-1177-2 (ebook)

Library of Congress Control Number: 2010901718

Printed in the United States of America

iUniverse rev. date: 04/13/2010

For the choir of angels

Contents

Foreword

As a young surgical resident, I was excited and walked with quickened pace when I saw the pink towers of the MD Anderson Cancer Center. Why did I have such an attraction to caring for these cancer patients? Certainly there was the challenge and complexity of the staging, treatment choices, and surgery. Integral was the hope of finding a "cure." There was a drive to help those stricken so randomly and often in the prime of life. But now, I believe I have the true answer to the strong appeal of specializing in the care of these remarkable individuals. It is the realization that cancer patients can teach us amazing coping skills and illuminate humanity's deep will to survive and embrace life.

Those stricken with cancer find a fierce desire to overcome their disease and resume their normal lives. Cancer's treatments make that struggle public. A breast cancer patient with advanced disease must decide whether life is worth losing her hair, perhaps a breast, or taking a pill that causes drenching sweats or vaginal dryness that can make considering sexual intimacy frightening. To survive, the cancer patient must, at least temporarily, navigate life stripped of physical beauty. The hair grows back but often finer and perhaps now gray. Chemotherapy treatments can reduce an athlete's drive to the simple goals of being able to spend a few hours upright or perhaps take a walk. On the other side of successful treatment, we see cancer patients restored to health and vigor. They are fully engaged in an active life and their physical beauty has returned. But they often find themselves changed from the inside out. They are transformed individuals with changed priorities and a far deeper appreciation for life. Old relationships are sometimes much stronger while others are no longer fulfilling, and so they are no longer nurtured. It is in this context that you should read this compelling book that tells the story of the breast cancer journey from every aspect, with humor and remarkable honesty.

Most breast cancer patients, like Jane, have not engaged in risky behavior that might provoke the onset of cancer. Yet, breast cancer so often strikes in midlife when a woman is enjoying that phase of defining the final and best chapters of her life. It is a time of great possibility. While some women with breast cancer have a family history of the disease, many do not. With routine breast self-examinations and screening mammograms, most breast cancer patients will present with early stage disease where mastectomy and chemotherapy are often unnecessary. Jane's story, however, exposes the disturbing reality that cancer shows no prejudice and will strike without warning. Despite having a large family with no history of breast cancer, Jane carefully followed every medical recommendation and maintained a healthy lifestyle only to find herself diagnosed with Stage III breast cancer requiring the most radical of treatments.

Dear reader, this is a story that sounds a universal bell and reaches out to touch a broad and committed audience. It is a story that opens our hearts and minds. It speaks to us. A great author is able to be truly honest and open. Jane Rudden demonstrates just such honesty in her memoir. She is not another celebrity facing this disease. She is an accomplished college professor who uses her academic skills and eloquent prose to reveal the complexity of this journey from every angle. Jane, a member of a remarkable Midwestern family of eleven children, lives far from any of her siblings. Her memoir chronicles the family dynamics as her siblings responded, each in his or her own way, to her crisis. Jane is a woman who, once wounded in love, is cautiously, but with hope, involved in a new romantic relationship when cancer strikes. Jane escorts the reader through her eventful journey with the rare lens of unabashed honesty. She details how plans for full-time work during treatment fade to meager hopes of being able to get up and walk without assistance and to stay optimistic while struggling with almost insurmountable exhaustion. Jane takes the reader through the most unexpected and greatest crisis of her life with insight, humor, and candor.

This is a book for any caregiver, whether in the medical profession, a family member, or a friend. Each of us can learn from this account how better to support our patients, our friend, or our family member who is dealing with cancer. I can assure you, dear reader, that the medical account presented is accurate and factual. However, this book should not be read as a primer on breast cancer treatment. Breast cancer is a heterogeneous disease with a spectrum of presentations requiring very different treatments. Fortunately, only a small proportion of those diagnosed with breast cancer will be diagnosed with as aggressive a form of breast cancer as Jane's. Read this rather as a remarkable life story beautifully told with humor and an incredible raw honesty. It is the story of how we reconcile our dreams, plans, and ambitions.

Daleela Getsiv Dodge, MD

Introduction

The American Cancer Society, Surveillance Research 2009, used the 1995-2005 incidence rates from forty-one U.S. states to estimate that 192,370 new cases of invasive breast cancer would be diagnosed in 2009-2010. An additional 62,280 women will be diagnosed with noninvasive breast cancer. Each of these women will look for answers, for coping strategies, for a reason why. They'll look to self-help books, memoirs written by breast cancer survivors, online sites, and medical dictionaries. Each will "come to grips" and then "get a grip" on the facts.

If We Must Dance, Then I Will Lead is one of the first books on breast cancer survival that combines memoir and health/science writing. I reach back to the yesterdays of my childhood to find the strength to endure my todays as a woman living with breast cancer. Explanations of medical terms and testing procedures are woven into the narrative to balance the unspeakably scary journey through a labyrinth of knives, needles, and radiation beams. A big dose of humor is added to soften the crippling starch of anxiety.

If We Must Dance, Then I Will Lead is one of the few books about breast cancer survival to include the point of view of sisters. I am one of seven sisters, in a family with no history of breast cancer. Though I was the one diagnosed with Stage IIIA breast cancer, my sisters are survivors, too. Nothing in our childhood prepared us for this crisis.

April 1, 2004 … no fooling. I'd discovered a lump the size of a golf ball, above the nipple of my right breast. I thought, *It wasn't on my mammogram three months earlier. It must be a pulled muscle from gardening. I'll give it the weekend to go away.* My doctor was alarmed and wasted no time finding answers. The next day I had a diagnostic mammogram and biopsy.

One week later, results of the biopsy showed cancer.

Two weeks after that, I celebrated my fifty-ninth birthday.

My diagnosis was an invitation to join an elite club. Membership required facing down my mortality. I reconciled myself with this early on. I had to in order to focus on what I had to do to regain my health. As Linda Ellerbee said, "Your first thought is not *will I lose my breast?* It's *will I lose my life?*"

I offer my story as a sprig of hope for newly diagnosed patients and their loved ones. Go bravely into the world of medical trappings that often lacks emotional support. Face down your fears with a glint in your eye. Stay informed. Look up the definitions of medical jargon. Read about typical courses of treatment and estimated survival rates. Ask loads of questions of your doctors and nurses. Hold onto hope. Keep a light heart. You are not alone in the fight. A choir of angels, populated by your family, friends, and fellow survivors, will swoop in and give you rest in the embrace of their wings.

Chapter One

We Interrupt This Life for Cancer—
Discovery and Diagnosis

Thursday, April 7, 2004—Monday, April 12, 2004

When the phone rang at midnight on the East Coast, I was already tucked in, exhausted from the sucker punch of the news that I had breast cancer.

"They've got the wrong girl!" said the caller.

My younger sister, Kate, the public defender, was calling from California. To say that Kate revels in finding justice for the common man would be a gross understatement. She once returned a ten-year-old skillet to a store for a refund because the bottom was warped and the grease puddled at the edges. The manager told her the store didn't carry that skillet any longer but would gladly exchange her old one for a different model. Now her days are spent in a courtroom negotiating jail time for felons, and her evenings, spent negotiating homework time, a jail of sorts, with her teenage son.

"Oh, Kate, you're too much," I mumbled in cottony half sleep. "I guess you talked with Christine and heard the news. I'm still reeling from the shock."

"You sound sleepy."

"It's midnight here, Kate."

"Well, I know, but I told myself this was a good enough reason to call so late."

I got up, threw on my robe, and went into the kitchen where I sat down at the table surrounded by all of my notes. The stove nightlight cast shadows on the wall as I reviewed the pathology with my sister and gave her some idea of what was next on the docket. Kate is the poster child for organization and generosity. She wasted no time with preliminaries.

"I'll get with Christine, and we'll figure out a travel schedule so somebody's with you for surgery and chemo. I can be there as soon as school is out." She further volunteered to get the word to the St. Louis family contingent and to my younger sister, Patti, who lived on the West Coast and kept in sporadic touch with family.

There are eleven siblings in my family—seven girls and four boys, most of them still living in the Midwest. Four of us, however, had roamed to the East and West Coasts, and the geographical distances between us, which had never mattered before, now came front and center. We had last circled the wagons of familial support at Mom's and at Dad's funerals. Mom died when she was fifty-eight years old from congestive heart failure. She'd also borne eleven surviving children, and her favorite snack was a Mounds bars chased down with Pepsi. Daddy died at seventy-three from lung cancer brought on by smoking no-filter cigarettes and rolling his own with Bull Durham. He'd set up shop at the head of the kitchen table and spread out the stock market page alongside a green glass ashtray. Bull Durham and a cup of reboiled coffee laced with Wilson's milk completed the tableau. If we'd had any guesses as to what would take us, we'd have put our money on Mom's heart condition.

My illness was an unexpected blow. I'd had my share of measles, mumps, chicken pox, and broken bones. Cancer had never been on the list of possible health setbacks. Daddy's cancer was self-imposed, after all. I'd gone through life believing I was the stalwart type, able to take on the challenges of sports, and later the challenges of balancing the stress of work with the rejuvenating effects of exercise. Someone else's bad news used to appear as a momentary blip on my screen, and I'd been grateful that their troubles hadn't been mine. I'd always taken my own health for granted—I had, but not anymore.

Only the week before I had sat in my doctor's office, legs dangling over the edge of the examination table, studying the circulatory system depicted on the oilcloth fellow mounted on the back of the door in an attempt to keep my mind off the purpose of my visit.

I had found the golf ball–size lump on April 1, 2004—no fooling—during a routine in-the-shower once-over. Soapy and slick made the perfect canvas for detection. *Must be a pulled muscle*, I thought. *A knot, not a lump, from gardening, or maybe my overenthusiastic practicing of the routines from the "Dumbbells for Smart People" workshop.* I thought, *I'll give it the weekend to go away.*

Lingering in the shower has always been an indulgence I savored. That day as the water streamed over me, I was lost in humming a tune resurrected from my unconscious. That's when I found it. Sensing the lump in my breast interrupted the chorus of "Crystal Blue Persuasion" and made my heart skip a beat. The abiding fear of the Big C closed my throat to any more humming.

§๛ ๛§

The rustle of my chart being removed from the holder on the outside of the door signaled that my turn had come. Doctor Susan swept into the room and greeted me with her usual enthusiasm.

She put me through a series of poses to detect the lump. First, I sat up straight facing her, and she looked from breast to breast to detect any differences in size or shape. Then she gently moved her hand over my right breast, from top to bottom, feeling for the lump. I hopped off the table and bent over at the waist to let gravity take over. My breasts hung down like pendulums, and there, protruding from the top of my right breast, was the lump. The dimensions were startling.

"The good news, Jane, is it came on quickly and is free moving. You had a clear mammogram in June and a clear exam in December," Doctor Susan explained. "It could be a plugged duct, but not likely. It could be a cyst, or it could be cancerous." I was mute, staring at the circulatory system fellow but seeing a future of unknowns.

Her face showed worry as she continued. "I don't like the way it feels. We don't usually see this in postmenopausal women. Let's get you in for a diagnostic right away." Before I left, Doctor Susan's nurse scheduled me for a diagnostic mammogram and possible biopsy at the hospital the next day.

Rather than wallow in the possible extreme, I stuffed my anxiety deep inside reason and headed to my appointment with Annie, my hairdresser. A little pampering was just what I needed.

Over the years, I'd freely experimented with my hair. The first time I'd had my hair frosted, I was a senior in high school and had silver highlights put into my brunette bob. The beauty shop was within walking distance of home, and as I came along the sidewalk toward the house, Daddy looked out the kitchen window and caught the first glimpse. As soon as I walked through the door, he said, in his trademark humor that usually missed the mark, "Oh, I thought that was Grandma walking down the street."

On the drive to the salon, I couldn't help but wonder whether today's appointment might be the last time in a long time that I'd have any hair to speak of, let alone to be the subject of a style debate.

When I arrived, Annie was snacking on oatmeal. As a devout athlete who competed in obstacle course events, she had not an ounce of fat on her body. She greeted me with her customary, "Hey, Jane, what are we doing today?"

I choked back the lump in my throat and said, "Well, I have news."

"Uh-oh. Is it bad news?" she asked.

"About a month from now, I don't think I'll have any hair at all," I whispered.

"Do you have cancer? What kind? My sister has cancer." It all spilled out of her like a litany.

"I'm having a biopsy tomorrow, but it doesn't look good. My doctor's treating it with urgency," I explained, dabbing my eyes.

"Don't you worry. This is the first day of your pampering yourself. My treat."

Her warm hug was interrupted by the UPS driver's, "Got a package here." The comic relief changed the mood, and Annie set to work on my hair.

I tried my best to focus on the pampering shampoo and cut, but my mind wouldn't cooperate. *Can't worry, Jane. Things will fall into place. Women survive this all the time.*

Then I thought of Ed. How would I break the news to him? Our romance was new—and worse, he was a breast man. My thoughts ran toward what I felt would be the worst possible outcome—a mastectomy.

After dinner that night, I casually mentioned the doctor's appointment to Ed and showed him the order for the mammogram and biopsy.

"This is scheduled for tomorrow," I told him. "I'm sure it's just routine."

"I didn't know anything about this. Why didn't you tell me?"

How could I when I was letting my infatuation with him override the obvious necessity of sharing the bad news with him? Months would pass before I let go of the fear that the only reason we were together was because I had all my parts.

§♋ ♋§

The next day I was ushered to a separate floor of the hospital's imaging center, away from the crowded waiting room on the first floor where women casually waited to be called for their routine mammograms. The diagnostic mammograms were performed upstairs, in an area with plush carpeting, a quiet waiting room with two or three women nervously paging through out-of-date magazines, and a long hallway of private rooms.

My films showed a large, shadowy mass that prompted an immediate hustle off to another of the private rooms along the hallway. Next step, an ultrasound-guided core biopsy. The air-conditioning in the spartan room nearly froze my undressed torso as I stretched out on the gurney. Just behind me, to the right, was a cart with an ultrasound screen and keyboard. See-through jars holding cotton balls, Q-tips, and sponges were lined up across the counter. Though comforting in their familiarity, they did nothing to distract me from the possibility of hearing bad news.

The hum of the fluorescent lights gave off a white noise that cut the deadening silence while I lay there shivering on the outside and trembling with anxious anticipation on the inside. I was in the company of three professionals. One was an R.N. who specialized in counseling newly diagnosed patients, though I didn't realize that was her role as she held my left hand and spoke in guarded terms about the possible diagnosis of breast cancer. Her sweet, round face was framed with curly brown hair that didn't quite hide the furrows in her brow. When she assured me there would be someone to guide me through the layers of appointments and decisions, I was stung by the inference. *Wait a second*, I thought, *let's see what the biopsy shows.* Another was a technician, whose efficiency assisting the radiologist inspired confidence in me. She talked me through the procedure and tilted the screen a bit so that I could see the searching eye of the ultrasound paddle. The third was the radiologist who performed the biopsy. She and the technician easily negotiated the steps in the procedure like long-time dance partners anticipating the other's next move. The nurse and technician remained cheerful but kept repeating the warning, "Stay away from the Internet."

They don't know who they're talking to, I thought. *I'm going to find out as much as I can about this beast as fast as I can. The minute I get home, I'm going to hit the Net running.* I strained my neck to see the screen as the radiologist guided the needle toward the mass. I wanted to watch everything that was happening—live. No blind obedience for me.

I had been injected with enough Novocain to tolerate the procedure without complaint, so I looked at the screen with a detached interest, as if that needle were going into someone else's body. The technician spread the cool gel on my breast with the seeing-eye paddle, slowly circling the targeted area of the lump until the radiologist said, "Hold it right there." She guided the needle, which reminded me of one of those old-timey ray guns, to the target. We all watched as the needle honed in on the mass, and I jumped like a scared kitten when the radiologist pulled the trigger. My three companions cheered with each successful plug of tissue extracted with the needle.

Once the procedure was over, I tried to engage the radiologist in idle chatter about what the ultrasound showed, but she didn't fall for it. Her answers were routine and formulaic.

"Sounds like you've done this a thousand times," I offered. "Any guesses as you looked at this mass?"

"Oh, we get a fair number of patients," she said. "We'll run some tests on these samples so you can have a preliminary report before you leave." Then she politely said, "Nice to meet you. Good luck," and left the room.

The technician hurried away to test the samples—five squiggly, opaque, wormlike forms lying on a sterile sponge—but before she left, she said, "See, these are the biopsy samples we just pulled. They look great. We'll have no trouble getting a good read from these." Then she leaned in and whispered, "I'm pretty sure it's cancer."

I stared at her with eyes widened in an effort to dam the impending tears. *I will not cry here. I will not be a predictably emotional woman who falls into a fit of hysteria.* I braced myself against the technician's completely inappropriate and unsolicited diagnosis, which she'd delivered with the casual air of "Fine weather we're having."

The R.N. excused herself, too, leaving me alone in that freezing room. Their routine procedure was my new experience. As they scurried off, not one of them looked back to see if I might need anything, such as a little comfort or reassurance. They just left me there, with my fear.

I'd made light of this procedure the night before when I told Ed what was going on and assured him I'd be okay on my own. After all, the appointment was supposed to be for a diagnostic mammogram, with a slim possibility that a biopsy might also be necessary. So, I'd dismissed his insistence on being with me, never dreaming I'd feel so adrift. *Baloney*, I thought. *I'm calling Ed. There's no sympathetic familiarity here for me.* I wrapped the gown around me and leaped off the gurney. In three strides, I was at the phone.

Ed and I had met at a karate studio three years earlier, at a time when I was determined to get myself together after a nasty divorce. I liked the dancelike movements of the martial arts, I wanted to bolster my self-confidence with self-defense, and I needed to get into shape after feeding my woes with cheese curls and old movies. Karate seemed a perfect solution. I was enthusiastic about this new venture but slightly nervous about showing up for the first class by myself. I had a feeling I'd be the oldest one in the class for beginners, but there was only one way to get started. I swallowed my pride, packed my crisp white uniform and belt into a duffel bag, and set out for a Tuesday night class for beginners, scheduled to start at eight o'clock.

The advanced students were involved in their class when I arrived. The walls echoed their *kihaps* as I dashed along the mirrored wall at the back of the studio and headed for the dressing room. *So far, so good.* The uniform was straightforward: white, starched, elastic-waist cotton pants and wraparound smocklike top. Barefoot and suited up, I went out into the studio looking for someone to help me tie the belt.

Partners were practicing their forms and self-defense moves, so I looked around for the instructor. Circulating among the students, critiquing their work and giving them pointers, was Ed, who looked over and caught my eye. He was working with a young black belt student. Ed wore a sweatband tied around his forehead and close-cropped dark hair. He was lean and all wrapped up in a bright white uniform that snapped with a starchy crispness as he moved. His uniform was tied at the waist with a black belt embroidered with his name and accented with two white stripes.

I approached him and bowed from the waist in deference as I had seen other students do. "Sir, could someone help me tie my belt? This is my first class." With a kind look devoid of all self-possession, Ed nodded to the young black belt student to help me.

When the beginner's class started, I was the only new student, so Ed gave me individual attention to set me on the right path. There was no rough or gruff response—just kindness.

I stuck with the karate classes for about a year and a half before I quit. At that time, Ed and I still only knew each other casually through class. But a year later, I ran into him at a convenience store. I remembered his manner as a karate instructor and the fondness I had harbored for him. I overcame my shyness and tapped on his truck window to say hi. To my surprise and secret delight, we chatted long enough to learn that each of us was single and wouldn't mind getting together to see a movie. We cautiously began navigating the waters of a new romance, convinced that commitment was not what either of us wanted—once burned, twice shy. And now, six months later, this.

"Hi, it's me. I'm at Women and Babies Hospital and just had the biopsy. It doesn't look good. The official results won't be ready until next week, but the technician suspects that it's cancer." Everything spilled out in one breath.

"Tell me which building you're in, and I'll be right there."

He left work on the spot and was in the waiting room when the biopsy trio told me I was free to go. Other than the unsolicited diagnosis given by the technician, the radiologist faxed a preliminary report to a surgeon, with whom I'd have an appointment before the day was out. As for the official results, I'd receive a call to set up an appointment with the radiologist. The emotion I'd refused to show in front of strangers came in a rush. I slouched onto Ed's shoulder and wept.

A technician led us to a private room off the waiting area and said, "I've been there. It'll be okay."

I wanted to whirl around on my heels and say, "This is not about you. I don't want to hear your story." But I held the words in check.

Ed and I sat in the private room knee-to-knee in facing parlor chairs. We held hands and waited to be told the time of our appointment with the surgeon. I was thrilled that I was going to have some of my questions answered. Within the hour, we were escorted to the surgeon's examining room, furnished with the requisite examining table, sterile cupboards and countertops, and two chairs. Moments later I was robed waist-up in a paper jacket with armholes that screamed, "Grand opening! Everyone welcome!" Ed sat on one chair, and I on the other, on top of my folded waist-up clothes.

The surgeon came in wearing a white coat starched to a fare-thee-well, reminiscent of Ed's starched karate uniform, but this white coat shouted trouble for me, an end to my control over everyday events. This white coat signified illness. The surgeon's name and credentials were machine-embroidered in red on the pocket, above his heart.

"Hello, I'm Dr. Surgeon. The radiologist faxed the preliminary report of your biopsy. Sit here, please, and I'll conduct a brief examination."

I settled myself on the exam table, which looked like an armless recliner in an almost completely flat position, and tried to engage him in a discussion of staging while he gently examined me.

"We can't stage it until after surgery," he said. "What the radiologist indicates is that it's a rather large mass and could possibly be a problem. See the receptionist at the desk and make an appointment for next week."

I was stunned. I had questions that couldn't wait a week.

Every time I'd taken a test in school, I wanted to know my score right away. After all that studying, I wanted to know if I got the answers right. Now here I was, armed with enough information to be dangerous about "if this is the stage, then such-and-such should happen," because I knew that staging was the key to treatment decisions. No matter how I asked the question, his response was the same: "We can't stage it until after surgery."

The sequence of tests, surgeries, and therapies was not clear to me, so I didn't realize I was asking preemptive questions. Nevertheless, I got from him the sense that I either should know or should wait in blind faith for the sequence to unfold. His bedside manner was too arrogant for me.

"Thank you, Dr. Surgeon, for seeing me on such short notice," I said, shaking his hand. My trembling was not from shivering this time but from frustration.

When we left the office, I told Ed, "That man will never touch me again."

We walked right past the receptionist's desk. My next call was to request a change of surgeons. Though grateful for his seeing me quickly, I was not inspired by his bedside manner. I wanted a surgeon who would recognize the earnest curiosity of my questions. I wanted a female.

The speed with which this drama was unfolding made me feel a little tipsy.

§ℜ ℜ₴

One week later, Ed and I waited in a parlor-type room furnished with catalog-coordinated furniture to hear the results of the biopsy. The place, which had apparently been decorated when the mauve and brown rage was in vogue, was so-so friendly for a not-so-pleasant conversation. The fact that we were there to hear bad news—the official results of the biopsy—was no secret. The sterility of the space shouted, "We can't tell you the diagnosis in the hallway or on the phone because we think you're going to make a big scene." *If these walls could talk,* I wondered, *how many echoes of women's frightened sobbing would trumpet from them?*

The radiologist who had performed the biopsy finally met us. R.N. Nan was there, too, as she was now officially assigned to guide me through the process. She stayed in the background, however, out of the limelight, waiting for a cue from the radiologist to "take it from here."

The radiologist seated herself with ramrod posture on the ottoman across from me. She wore a tiny, stiff neck scarf to accent the black pantsuit. Short, short hair crowned her. In staccato, she said, "It is not good news. It is cancer." She went on to relate the pathology report's gross description. "Right breast—Received in formalin are five cylindrical cores of variegated yellow adipose tissue and dense white soft tissue measuring 0.15 centimeters in diameter and ranging from 1.3 to 1.6 centimeters in length. There are also bits of soft tissue present measuring 0.3 centimeters in greatest dimension. 5+Bits/1/NS, long."

I absorbed the blow with as much dignity as I could muster, thinking, *How could this be? Just last week everything was fine.* My forbidden Internet searches had armed me with a list of questions. Asking them grounded me against bursting into tears. "What is the exact type of cancer? What stage is it? Please explain in terms I can understand."

"In your case," she read from the report, "'infiltrating and in situ mammary carcinoma. Focally, the infiltrating carcinoma demonstrates squamous cell carcinoma differentiation, suggesting metaplastic carcinoma.' We won't be able to stage it until after surgery."

No elaboration was offered, and these were not terms I understood, so I pressed on. "Has the cancer spread to the lymph nodes?"

Cue the R.N.

"R.N. Nan has a lot of experience with this," the radiologist said, "and will be able to answer your questions." Then she stood, offered her hand in a farewell shake, said good luck, and left the room.

This was the first of many times I'd be summarily handed over to a nurse or technician for more information. I came to believe that there was a silent gunshot that started the race to see patients and an invisible whip that cracked at the doctors' heels to keep those billable hours mounting.

Indeed, R.N. Nan knew all the answers and patiently wrote them on the now sweat-rippled paper I'd been folding and unfolding while the radiologist was there. Our give-and-take went something like checking answers on a pop quiz in the eighth grade. First on the list was a three-part question: "What type of cancer do I have, what stage is it, and what does that mean in my case?"

R.N. Nan wrote, "Infiltrating duct carcinoma—stage determined after surgery." She couldn't address the seriousness of the cancer (staging) or whether or not the disease had spread to the lymph nodes or other organs. "We'll only know about metastasis after the lymph nodes are removed." All of these terms were coming at me in rapid fire. My reading in books and on the Web sites had armed me with enough information to grasp the general idea of what R.N. Nan was saying.

"What about additional tests to see if it's spread?" I asked.

"We will get labs, chest x-rays, and a bone scan," R.N. Nan said, "which will check for the disease in bones and lungs. You may need CT scans, but we're not sure yet."

"What are my treatment choices? What is recommended and why?" I pressed on.

"You will be scheduled for surgery for either a lumpectomy or mastectomy. Either surgery will include lymph node removal."

I was barely remembering to breathe. "What are the risks and side effects of the different treatments after surgery?"

"With radiation therapy, there is a sunburn-type effect to the skin and mild fatigue. If you need chemotherapy, there is nausea and sometimes vomiting, hair loss, and fatigue. If you are a candidate for antiestrogen therapy—which relies on selective estrogen receptor modulators, or SERMs—the side effects are medication dependent. Tamoxifen and Arimidex are two examples of antiestrogen therapy drugs."

"How long will each course of treatment last?" I asked.

"Radiation therapy will last about six or seven weeks, Monday through Friday, but no weekends or holidays. Chemotherapy depends on the final pathology report regarding lymph node involvement."

Among my worries was missing work. I was teaching at a local university and was eligible to apply for promotion to full professor that fall. I'd been chasing dreams all my life just for the thrill of accomplishment, and I couldn't help thinking that this nasty little tumor would be an interruption in my plans. I continued with the Q and A with R.N. Nan.

"Will I be out of work? For how long?" I had begun to realize the comfort of routine in my life, and the impending disruption was unnerving.

R.N. Nan said, "It depends on the surgery option. It could be one to four weeks."

"Will I be able to drive myself home after treatment?" I was afraid that not being able to drive would compromise my independence and I'd just be thought of as *the cancer patient.* My mom learned to drive when she was in her fifties; the freedom and independence opened up a whole new world for her as she gallivanted at will with the grandchildren without having to call upon anyone else. Having witnessed that metamorphosis in her made me appreciate the benefits of driving that I'd always taken for granted, and I worried that my treatment might make *me* the dependent one.

"After radiation, yes, you'll be able to drive," R.N. Nan clarified. "If you have chemotherapy, however, you'll need someone to drive you for the first treatment. If you tolerate the drugs okay, then you may drive yourself to and from chemotherapy. You'll, of course, need a ride to and from the hospital for surgery."

My questions continued. "What are the chances of this cancer coming back after the recommended treatment?"

R.N. Nan skirted the finer details of this question by saying, "It depends on lymph node results from surgery and the treatment given."

"Should I follow a special diet with this treatment?"

"No," she said, "eat a well-balanced diet."

"In my case," I asked, "what kinds of breast reconstruction are possible?"

"If you have a mastectomy, you can have an immediate implant reconstruction or a TRAM reconstruction, which uses your abdominal muscle and tissue for the reconstructed breast. There is no reconstruction necessary with a lumpectomy." Despite this being a decision I wouldn't have to make for many months, R.N. Nan's patience prevailed.

For my big finish, I asked, "What are the chances of survival based on this cancer, as you see it?"

"It appears that the survival rate is very good," she began. "But we need more information from the surgery report to be more accurate."

I was satisfied, for the time being, having these somewhat sketchy answers to my questions. The absence of information wasn't R.N. Nan's fault. She wasn't a doctor. She knew only what she knew, and what she'd been able to offer was enough for me, a patient dizzy with the news of a cancer diagnosis. She encouraged me to call her if I had any more questions or if she could help in any way. Her first assignment—find a female surgeon for me.

Another worry that needled me was jeopardizing the romance with Ed. The blush was still on the rose, but I couldn't pretend that early euphoria would be enough to see us through what looked, at this point, like a long battle—a battle with threats and scars I couldn't begin to imagine. I braced myself to give Ed every chance to run for his life, but his intuitions beat me to the punch. As we left the building after the session with R.N. Nan, he stopped in the middle of the sidewalk, turned me to face him, and hugged me right then and there.

"I'm so sorry," he whispered in my ear. "We'll get through this."

"No one signs up for this, Ed. Please, make your escape now. I'll completely understand."

"Going through things alone has got to stop," he said, putting an end to the debate. As if the diagnosis hadn't been enough to bring the tears, those words tipped the scales.

§☙   ❧

Armed with Puffs tissues, chardonnay, and all the notes from R. N. Nan and the radiologist, Ed and I headed for my back porch to make the calls to my family. The screened-in porch had dark green shutters on the north side to block out any wild weather central Pennsylvania might serve up and provided some privacy from the way-too-close neighboring deck typical of townhouses. On that day more than ever, the porch was an island of calm. Ed dialed my sister, Christine, and I took a long pull on the chardonnay.

Women have a reservoir of calm and reason that they tap into in the face of threat and tragedy. I've admired that trait in my mother and sensed the same thing in my sisters, yet I was surprised to discover that the reservoir was part of me as well. An inner switch was thrown, and I faced the diagnosis like a homework assignment. This unwanted threat to my life would not win without a fight. And to name the threat was to know the threat, and, by golly, this hellish thing *was* going to have a name.

"Will I get to talk to Jane?" Christine asked Ed.

"Why, sure. I just wanted to ease the anxiety for her and make the call."

I took the phone and skirted the fragile emotions I sensed at the edge of Christine's voice by launching into medical mumbo jumbo. She was ahead of the curve with this news because we'd chatted a week earlier about the impending biopsy and the possibility of a cancer diagnosis. Being an R.N. manager in the Department of Medicine at a southeastern university, she was my logical choice for a sounding board. She assured me that we had no family history of breast cancer, that lumpectomies produce good results, and that mastectomies should be avoided whenever possible. The skin could be preserved and the tumor removed, she said, and if I did end up needing a mastectomy, reconstruction would follow right on the heels of chemo. *Oh, God, chemo!*

I read the details of the pathology report as I would have read a grocery list—even a pretense of mental distance was comforting. This was her area of expertise and therefore some consolation for having to talk about this at all.

The presence of squamous cell carcinoma caught her attention. "That doesn't belong there," she pointed out. "Squamous cells are present in the upper layer of the skin, not in breast tissue."

I could tell that the inner switch was thrown for Christine, too. A calm came over her, and she began an impromptu recitation of a possible time line for surgeries and treatment.

"Would you come and be with me for the surgery?" I asked. "And for a few days after? I need your medical eyes and ears."

"Of course. All I'm doing is taking summer classes, and I have loads of vacation time from work. Don't worry, I'll work it out," she promised.

"Would you call Kate for me and fill her in on everything?" I was exhausted and didn't think I could get through another lengthy phone call with the same level of control—or anything even close to it. My skin was thin under my crusty shell of competence. I could cry on cue.

Chapter Two

Tunnel Vision—Preoperative Testing

Tuesday, April 13, 2004—Tuesday, April 20, 2004

"Have you ever been in that tube, Doctor?" I asked.

"You will find that I am an empathetic physician. I went kicking and screaming to my own hysterectomy," she answered. "My colleagues had a fight persuading me."

"Have you ever been in that tube, Doctor?" I asked again.

She threw a glance at R.N. Nan. "I'm going to have trouble with this one."

No bigger than a minute, my new surgeon, Dr. Dee, inspired confidence. She was dressed in a skirt, a sweater, and a pair of heels, with a small jade cross on a gold chain around her neck serving as her only adornment. She was reputed to be a leader in the field of breast cancer surgery who believed in breast conservation. She was thorough, minced no words, and remained cautiously optimistic about conserving the breast.

"The mass is big," she pointed out, "but its placement at twelve o'clock, above the nipple, is in our favor. It's possible to remove the tumor without sacrificing the breast. Surgery should be as soon as possible after the preoperative testing." She looked to R.N. Nan and rattled off the list of necessary tests. "I want a CT scan, a chest x-ray, a bone scan, and an MRI. Set her up to see Hematology, Radiation, and Cosmetics." She was confident and efficient in shuffling reports and x-rays, and in fielding my questions. Despite her heavy patient load, I felt I could take all the time I needed with my questions. The repartee was brisk and on point but not rushed.

ॐ   ॐ

One of the first books I read about breast cancer was McCarthy and Loren's *Breast Cancer? Let Me Check My Schedule!* Ten women working outside their homes tell their stories about "fitting breast cancer into their very busy lives." Are we so indispensable, or have we made ourselves so, that an illness as threatening as cancer can't persuade us to pay attention to ourselves? In the foreword of the book, Erma Bombeck admits, "I was a lot like Amy in the book, who, when her gynecologist warned her that lumps in her breast suggested a mammogram, got dressed, added this item to the Filofax under 'medium level priority' item number eleven, and went back to the office."

Determined to keep my professional persona intact, I doggedly completed my teaching semester. On the day of the CT scan, I ran upstairs to my office during a class break and chug-a-lugged the second of three Prepcat drinks. The label said the flavor was strawberry but didn't mention anything about the chalky aftertaste. The scan was scheduled for the end of the school day, and the instructions were pretty specific about when to drink the first and the second doses. I was supposed to wait until just before the scan before drinking the third.

I'd awakened that morning in a cold sweat, dreaming with palpable fear that I was being rolled into an MRI tube and that I was incapable of putting mind over matter. By six o'clock that morning I was on the phone with Virginia Jan, my best friend and lung cancer patient herself. She talked me down off the ledge of fright.

"Don't let that machine scare you," she said. "I've had every scan known to man, and the CT scanner looks like a big open donut. The gurney is rolled right through it, and you won't feel confined. The process is painless and quick."

The testing area was on the hospital's basement level. When I got off the elevator, I was met with teeming crowds of people bustling in and out of the cafeteria, transport personnel navigating gurneys through the throngs and on toward the testing area, and Ed. He was standing over against the wall at the near end of the long hallway where I was to report for the test. He'd slipped out of work for an hour or so to be with me at the onset of the testing. I felt my face light up at the sight of him. Virginia Jan had calmed my nerves about the machinery used for the test, and now Ed's presence quelled any remaining anxiety. But there were still a few surprises.

Two young male technicians took charge of the CT scan with clipped directives.

"Drink down the last of the Prepcat," one of them said.

"Lie down on the gurney, feet toward the wall, and we'll begin," said the other.

You don't scare me, I thought. *You look like my nephews.*

"When I inject the contrast dye," one of the nephew look-alikes said, "it's going to feel like you're wetting yourself."

"Thanks for the warning," I commented. Sure enough, memories of enuresis washed warmly over me, and visions of dark-rimmed, yellow pools on the mattress danced in my head.

Other than the contrast dye, the scan was noninvasive and stress free. The mechanized gurney rolled forward through the donut hole up to my ribs and then backed out. The goal was to see if the cancer had spread to vital organs in the abdominal and pelvic regions.

One of the technicians asked why I was having the scan. I said, "It's preoperative to breast cancer surgery."

His face sagged as if he were thinking, *Aw, I'm so sorry*. But he just said, "All the best," and extended a handshake. He looked a bit disarmed. Perhaps I reminded him of his auntie.

After the CT scan, I was sent straight down the hall to x-ray, where three other gown-wrapped women waited in the row of chairs out in the main hallway. No one spoke. The realization slowly dawned on me that this road map of testing would create silent comrades for me in the fight against cancer. I couldn't, however, initiate any chatter. I was exhausted and wide-eyed with anticipation of the results of each of these tests. We knew each other was there and, for now, stayed still in our reflections. After a wait made to feel longer by the group silence, my name was called. It was my turn.

"Hi! My name is Melanie," the x-ray technician said. "This will only take a few minutes." She was young and chipper, giving her job her all as she gently guided me through the steps. "Stand right up against the machine. Rest your chin on the top. Put your hands on your hips. Lean your elbows forward. Breathe in and hold your breath until I tell you."

"All right, dear," I said.

"Why are you having a chest x-ray?" Melanie asked.

"It's preoperative to breast cancer surgery," I said, echoing my pat answer and expecting that this explanation wasn't out of the ordinary in this business. Instead, she teared up and said, "I'm so sorry. I didn't know."

My armor was chinked. Her compassion forced me to choke back my own tears and swallow hard. The buffer of distance I had worked to maintain between these tests and the fact that this was actually me going through them was beginning to lose strength.

"Oh, thank you, dear," I said to her. "Now, you *are* doing self-breast exams, aren't you? That's the way I found my lump."

"Well," she said shyly, "I try to remember, but I don't always."

"Just a quick once-over when you're soapy and slick in the shower. It doesn't take a minute," I suggested.

"I will," she promised. "I wish you the best of luck."

Day one of testing was over, and I was exhausted from the emotional drain that snuck up on me.

§♫ ♫§

Day two's agenda began with an early morning pre–bone scan injection.

"There's just a trace of radioactive medicine in this shot," said the nurse. "It won't hurt you at all."

Then why is it in a triple-lined lead container, snuggled into a custom-built Styrofoam bed? And why are you wearing a lead apron and gloves that look like cartoon oven mitts?

I reported two and a half hours before the scan for the injection of a radioactive substance that would spread through my bloodstream and cause my bones to light up under the scanner camera. My instruction then was to drink several glasses of water to help eliminate any of the substance not picked up by the bones. There was no discomfort and very little preparation on my part, so I used those two and a half hours to meet with a cosmetic surgeon.

His office was a gallery of simple line drawings of women's torsos, much like I'd seen in the pages of nearly every book I'd read—lumpectomy scar, right mastectomy scar, left mastectomy scar, bilateral mastectomy scar. I didn't identify myself with the drawings at all. Those weren't real women, and those sketches had nothing to do with me.

Dr. Cosmetics did not stand on ceremony. "Since this is a consultation preceding surgery," he said, "I'll show you the reconstruction options, should that become necessary." He wore a light tan shirt, sleeves rolled up to the elbows, and a brown tie. His slacks were a dark tan, belted with brown leather and fastened high above his waist. We sat at one end of a long conference table surrounded by walls of shelves holding medical volumes.

"I'm scheduled for a lumpectomy, but Dr. Dee wanted me

to make the rounds of all possible medical players," I explained, hoping to warm his cool reception.

"This is a silicone sack filled with saline, or salt water," he said without responding to my comment as he handed me a display model. I'd never held anything that gelatinous before, and I found the lava lamp tide a bit disconcerting. "An empty silicone sack, or expander, is implanted under the skin and muscle at the time of the mastectomy," he went on. "After surgery, you come into the office every week for an injection of saline through a valve that projects from the sack through your skin. Over a period of several weeks, the expander is brought to the size and shape you want for the reconstructed breast. Then this expander has to be removed. It's an in-office procedure. We remove the expander, insert the permanent implant, and perform nipple and areola reconstruction."

"Oh, is that how it works? I'm not wild about the idea of having a foreign object in my body. That's not for me," I said, vetoing that plan.

"Another choice is the latissimus dorsi, or back flap," he continued. "The back muscle, the latissimus dorsi, along with an eye-shaped wedge of skin, are rotated from the back to the breast site and sutured in place." Dr. Cosmetics sketched a female back and the route to the breast site with his fountain pen. "The tissues and muscle moved from the back remain attached to their original blood supply. That decreases the possibility of necrosis."

"Necrosis?"

"Death of the cells," he uttered without affect. "Of course, you'd be left with a scar on your back."

"Yes, I see."

"The TRAM flap," he went on, explaining option three, "uses the fat and skin from your lower abdomen to form a new breast." The fountain pen bled onto the page as Dr. Cosmetics made a rudimentary sketch of the procedure. "TRAM stands for transverse rectus abdominous myocutaneous muscle. There are two major muscles that run north and south on your abdomen. We remove a football-shaped section of your lower abdomen, skin and fat, and tunnel it under your skin along with one of the muscles. The mastectomy scar is reopened, and the flap is pushed out of it and formed into a breast mound. Flesh and muscle are sutured in place. Here again, the flap remains connected to its original blood supply. You'll hear this procedure called the tummy tuck because the belly fat is removed."

I heard tummy tuck and said, "Why not? A tummy tuck at no extra charge."

He wrote, "Prefers TRAM."

"How many of these procedures do you perform in a year's time, Dr. Cosmetics?" I asked.

He shrugged his shoulders and said, "It's hard to say."

"Could I speak with any of your former patients?" I asked.

"Sure, just ask the receptionist on your way out."

"Are you a participating provider with the ABC Insurance Company?" I asked.

"I think so. I know we don't get nearly the full amount for the work we do," he muttered.

"Well, the lumpectomy is next week. If all goes well, I won't be seeing you again. But, I thank you very much for your time and expertise. Dr. Dee highly recommended you," I said, trying to wrap up this meeting as quickly as possible.

"You're welcome. Good luck." He offered his hand in a farewell shake.

By the time my appointment with Dr. Cosmetics was over, the nuclear medicine was fully circulating in my bones. As I returned for the bone scan, I started feeling slightly anxious that I might become claustrophobic under the scanner. But my reading about this procedure had originally convinced me I would be okay and would not creep out, so I lay down on my back on the cold table, sandwiched between that hard layer and the scanner that would pass slowly over my body, closed my eyes, and tried my best to relax.

"No peeking," the female technician teased. "Are you okay?"

"I'm fine," I said not so convincingly.

"The camera will be over your face for a very short period of time and then will reverse down your body," she assured me.

I froze in place, the way we did as kids when we played Swing the Statue. Whoever was "it" gave each player a swing around, and when released, the player struck a pose and then froze like a statue. When everybody had been swung and was frozen, the object of the game was to change positions without letting the person who was it catch you. If he or she did, you'd be it.

The camera skimmed the surface of my body to check my entire skeleton for any spread of the disease to the bones. When the lens skimmed over my head, I opened my eyes a little only to see that my head was the baloney in the sandwich of table and camera.

The very second the camera cleared my face and moved back toward my feet, I turned my head to the side to look at the screen. The images looked like Halloween skeleton cardboard cutouts, except these were my bones. As I lay there gazing at the screen, an old joke popped into my head: "Why did the x-ray technician marry the homely girl? Because he was the only one who could see anything in her."

I knew the radioactive medicine illuminated the bones, so the fact that mine were lit up like neon wasn't a surprise. But there were brighter spots, hot spots, along my shins. The hushed conversation between the technician and her colleague behind a glass enclosure made my heart race.

"Let's reposition you to focus only on your forearms," the technician said, helping me up and off the table. "We called downtown for an immediate read of your scan. If your forearms glow as brightly as your shins, there's a possibility the disease has spread."

I sat in a desk chair pulled up as close to the table as I could, straddled my knees around the chair, and snuggled up even closer. I leaned forward and placed both arms, palm-side up, on the table. This positioned me with my back to the screen, so I couldn't follow the scan and look for hot spots. I leaned my forehead against the suspended camera and thought, *Dear God, is this it? Of all places, in the bones! And, of all things, had my best intentions to stay healthy through heavy exercise weakened my bones and invited in cancer?*

Thankfully, the forearm scan did not glow like my shins. The explanation was that, in an effort to exercise my way to a healthier me for recovery, I had over walked and had developed shin splints. The technician's prescription was straightforward: "Stop walking until it stops hurting. Wait one more week. Return to walking at one-half mile per walk, and always walk on a cushioned track."

My athletic past flashed before me. I was disappointed to learn that my legs, which had taken me around the bases in a grand slam home run, and had seen me through spike after spike in the volleyball city playoffs, and had sped me up and down the basketball court as a roving forward, and had danced the night away at Teen Town, were now copping out on me. St. Anthony's gymnasium had been the scene for all our high school indoor sports. In our small all-girls Catholic school, grades kindergarten through eight were on the first floor, and the high school classrooms were upstairs. The gymnasium occupied the two-story hollow in the middle of the building. Basketball games were played after school, with opposing teams busing in from neighboring parishes. We didn't have any special uniforms. We wore our gym clothes—pale yellow one-piecers with cap sleeves, a flared skirt to mid-thigh, and matching bloomers. Although those clothes were sweaty and wrinkled from the week's classes, we would shake them out and wear them for the games. Give me the grime of the basketball court any day to all this anticipation and worry. I'd even take that little spitfire from Holy Angels Parish, whose guarding technique included giving me a rat-a-tat series of punches in the stomach and back.

§☙ ☙§

Day three of preoperative testing brought the most feared test of all—the dreaded MRI. When Dr. Dee had originally listed all the necessary tests I'd need to complete, I'd blanched when she said, "And an MRI." I'd heard and read a lot of unpleasant stories about the MRI, and the specter of that tube gave me pinpricks of claustrophobia that raised the hair on my arms.

"Could I have a relaxant to see me through?" I'd asked. "And would it be possible for me to see that chamber of horrors ahead of time, so I could perhaps get over my anxiety?"

A nod toward R.N. Nan and my requests were granted. Dr. Dee wrote a prescription for one Valium, and R.N. Nan arranged for a guided tour the day before the test. The MRI technician was gracious, explaining the entire process and telling me that I could bring along a favorite CD to be piped through the earphones. As I was leaving the tour, I noticed a photo on the wall that showed the MRI technicians looking into an empty tube, with the caption, "Did we leave a patient in there?" Glib MRI humor didn't help settle my jitters, but the tour had been very helpful.

On the day of my test, while waiting to be called for my turn in the MRI tube, Ed and I paged halfheartedly through magazines. A technician was loitering nearby, straightening the magazines and looking like she was just killing time.

"What test are you here for?" she asked me. "I checked the list, and there are no more mammograms scheduled this afternoon."

"It's a preoperative breast MRI," I answered.

"I'm a breast cancer survivor." she replied immediately. "It was really tough. But look at me now," she added, apparently trying to reassure me.

I said nothing. Blinded by the unknowns that lay ahead, I couldn't engage in chatter about others' stories. About that time a nurse called my name, and I followed her back to the dressing room, leaving Ed to deal with the technician. He told me later about the conversation they had.

"I don't think it's appropriate to mention the rough road ahead to someone who's just going through the preliminaries," he had told her.

"Oh," she'd said, taken aback. "I only wanted to tell her things would get better—"

"You heard her say pre-op," Ed had interjected. "It's upsetting enough for her right now. So, just keep that in mind."

"I'm so sorry," she said. "I meant no harm." End of drama. Exit the technician. But that was a perfect example of something I'd already learned: When dealing with new cancer patients, words need to be as carefully chosen as the timing of when those words are spoken—and medical professionals can be among the most insensitive.

For the breast MRI, I was positioned tummy-side down on a mechanized gurney no wider than the hollow of the MRI tube. I opened my gown and let "the girls" fall into a plastic well below the surface of the bed. My forehead rested on a cushioned bolster, and my arms were down at my sides. An IV was inserted into my left arm to accept the contrast dye that would be injected halfway through the test. And judging from the calm that was washing over me, my little Valium capsule was working.

I'd given the technician a Jazz Masters CD and put a card from Ed at the bottom of the well platform so I could see the words during the MRI.

You can!
Whatever you're faced with, you can handle.
Whatever you're feeling, you can cope.
Whatever you fear, you can conquer
As long as you believe in yourself …
… As much as I believe in you.

With everything in place and with me feeling plenty mellow, I said, "Let's do it."

"We're going to," the technician said, taking her place at the control board behind a glass partition.

The gurney slowly rolled into the MRI tube, but all I saw was the card. *This is great,* I thought. *I have no sense of being enclosed. I can do this.*

"How are you doing in there?" I heard the technician's voice ask through the earphones.

"Fine," was all I answered. *Let's not stop for chitchat.*

After roughly five minutes, out rolled the gurney for the injection of the dye. I didn't feel a thing. Back into the MRI tube I rolled, this time for a period of about eleven minutes of clinking, clanking, and knocking while the machine took pictures of the girls from every angle.

"You're doing great," encouraged the technician. "Just three more minutes."

For a long time before that test, I'd been keeping a list of things I wanted to accomplish and a list of things I didn't think I could ever do. On that second list was "Have an MRI and put mind over matter." And yet there I was, doing exactly that.

After I rejoined Ed in the waiting room, he said, "When you didn't come out within the first few minutes, I figured everything was okay and you were going through with it."

"Yeah," I whispered, "the Valium relaxed me." I wept with relief as we walked past the lobby fountain glittering with coins that had been thrown by all the hopefuls who'd come before me.

§♌   ♌§

There were two more appointments to keep in order to complete Dr. Dee's list: Radiology and Hematology.

Dr. Radiologist's nurse took a Polaroid picture of me and stapled it to the outside of my chart. Ed sat patiently beside me while I answered all the requisite questions. There was a lot of writing, hole punching, and stapling going on. Once the preliminaries were over, Dr. Radiologist (another nephew look-alike) joined us in the exam room. His manner was disarming, and I took that as an invitation to reel off my questions at will.

"Why do I have breast cancer? You have to give me a hook here and I'll stop asking. There's no family history, and I've always been a specimen of good health." He appeared to be genuinely listening as I pleaded my case.

"You're not going to get an answer because there is no answer. Too many environmental factors could be at play," he offered as he rolled his chair back against the wall. He leaned back, crossing his right ankle over his left knee. I think he could sense that I'd done enough reading to be dangerous but was savvy enough to check the validity of what I'd read against what he knew. His manner was lacking any patronizing overtones, and this endeared him to me.

We discussed the time line of treatments and where radiation fit into the scheme. This was a preliminary visit and I wouldn't see him again until after the lumpectomy, when he would examine my skin and determine its ability to withstand radiation.

§୧   ୧୫

The following Tuesday, April 20, I met with the hematology oncologist. She would be the final member of my medical team, and the purpose of this visit was to discuss the options for delivering chemo, in the event the pathology indicated the need.

Dr. Oncologist came striding into the exam room, hand extended in greeting. She was young, tall, and slender, with her brunette hair styled in a very short pixie cut. She wore a flowing floral-print dress and red Mary Janes. I interpreted this everyday look to be her way of saying, "White coats create too much distance between you and me." I felt perfectly at ease. If she were anything like Dr. Dee and Dr. Radiologist, she'd answer all of my questions and let me partner with her in the therapy phase.

Ed and I sat on the two chairs at the foot of the exam table. The room was so small that accommodating the cabinets, the brochure rack, and the giant step-on scale—guaranteed to show you that your bathroom scale is five pounds light—was a tight squeeze. R.N. Nan, who stayed back by the door, was there as an escort and for moral support.

Dr. Oncologist pulled up the rollaway stool. She, Ed, and I

made a cozy little trio, with the exam table doubling as a desk for my flimsy file. The doctor was very engaging, so I began by asking all my questions. She hinted at the benefits of neoadjuvant therapy.

"Successful neoadjuvant chemotherapy will shrink the tumor before surgery, making it easier to remove. It's nice for me to see the tumor shrink, but I always wonder if there were tiny cells left behind," she said.

I wasn't up to speed on the term "neoadjuvant," despite all the reading I'd done. R.N. Nan always responded to my questions, but she seldom volunteered information. I often knew what the doctors were talking about only because I'd read about it. I listened with great interest to the ins and outs of neoadjuvant care, but, frankly, I couldn't put all the pieces together.

"So, is that like a clinical trial?" I asked innocently.

She slapped my file onto the exam table and snapped, "No, I have no clinical trials going on in the treatment room!"

Raw nerve alert! I recoiled to create a bit more distance between us. *What is this all about?* I wondered. *Is she threatened by my questions? I thought we were just discussing various approaches.* I was stunned but decided to drop the matter and move on.

After the appointment I told Ed that I wasn't sure I'd be comfortable with Dr. Oncologist. Her reaction to my question about the clinical trial was intimidating.

"Call R.N. Nan and ask her about the best way to make a change," Ed advised. "She'll understand."

"It shouldn't be my problem to sort out these doctors. I'm exhausted from managing information," I said. "It may be routine for them, but how could they think I already know all there is to know?"

Chapter Three

Measure Twice, Cut Once—The Lumpectomy

Thursday, May 6, 2004—Sunday, May 9, 2004

Christine drove up from North Carolina to be with me for the lumpectomy. It was a long nine hours in the car before she swooped up my driveway in Pennsylvania. As I walked out to greet her, we exchanged waves. Her wide smile did little to hide the tears pooling in her eyes. "I'm glad to see you, but I hate the reason I'm here," she managed to whisper. I detected a crack in her voice as she embraced me tightly.

"It's okay, Christine. I'm fine. It'll all be fine." I rescued her from the emotional upset with a return squeeze, a gentle rub on her back, and the only words I knew to say.

Her voice shuddered ever so slightly as, on the wind of a sigh, she said, "You're a lot calmer than I am—and I over packed, as usual."

"Well, let's get all that luggage inside. Cute blouse," I said in an effort to break the tension. "Geez, Christine, you look great. You cut your hair, and that's a different color, isn't it?" Her blond short cut was accented with coppery tones along the bangs.

"Yeah, I'm trying something new. I put a little of the coloring mousse on my fingertips and then wisped it through my hair to give it a highlighted look exactly where I wanted it."

"It looks good. I guess I won't be worrying about that for a while," I chuckled.

"Oh, Jane, I didn't mean to bring that up. Listen to me going on about my hair."

"It's okay. And you didn't bring it up. I did."

Christine took a deep breath and let it out slowly. "Well, since we're talking about it, here, I got you these two hats."

"Cute! I'll hang them on the front hall mirror, ready to wear," I said. We left her luggage at the foot of the stairs and went straight through the kitchen to the screened back porch. It was beastly hot, in the 90s with no promise of relief for the next few days, but the shade from the tall maples out back helped cool the porch. With tall glasses of iced lemonade in hand, we sat in the wicker chairs and chatted.

"I really appreciate your making the trip, Christine. I'm still in a bit of shock over this whole thing. I keep bugging the doctors to give me a reason why."

"I thought about that, too, Jane. On the trip up, a checklist ran through my mind. I had my MapQuest printout and a big coffee, so I just let the miles roll by and had a good think. No family history of breast cancer. Daddy's lung cancer was self-imposed. Mom's heart condition was always the health concern most expected to visit the next generation. I'm thinking the source of your breast cancer had to be the coal furnace, or maybe breathing Daddy's secondhand smoke."

Daddy drove the owl run—from eleven at night until seven in the morning—on the Carondelet bus line and spent his off-hours sitting at the end of the kitchen table studying the stock market reports (without a penny invested), drinking coffee, and smoking. He rolled his own cigarettes, deftly tapping the Bull Durham into the finger-creased tissue paper. He'd cinch the pouch closed with his teeth and use both hands to pack and roll the cigarette. A lick of the tip of his tongue across the tissue, a quick twist on one end to form a wick, the open rolled end between his lips—that cigarette, chased down with boiled coffee laced with Wilson's condensed milk, was dessert to Daddy.

"I didn't think of the furnace and Daddy's smoking. You'd think it would be lung cancer if anything," I commented. "Did you have any problems getting a few days off from work? This was pretty last minute."

"You know," she said, "I ran into my boss in the parking lot and asked him right then and there about taking a few days off. When I told him the reason why, his voice got sort of soft, and he told me to do what I needed to do and that he'd be thinking about us."

"Thank goodness for that. You need peace of mind that everything's okay at home while you're here," I said.

"This isn't fair," Christine said. "Your illness is too close. You're sandwiched between my nurse-ness and my heart."

"You're my sister, that's first. The bonus for me is that you know the medical terminology. I don't expect you to ignore the closeness," I said.

"I feel like I have amnesia for everything I've learned about oncology. My grip on the medical side of me is slipping."

"Let's take it one step at a time," I said. "The diagnosis is totally unexpected, and letting the news sink in is going to take awhile. Let's change the subject for a minute. We have an assignment. You know that Kate is allergic to my cats." Kate starts to sound like a husky-voiced Mae West within an hour of being in my home. "So she called around to find a room where she could stay while she's in town. She found one nearby, and I told her we'd check it out."

§꩜   ꩜§

Lucy, the landlady, met Christine and me in her driveway, and after exchanging courtesies, we began the tour at the garage's side door. "Now, the room has a private entrance through the garage. I'm very particular about keeping the doors locked," she explained.

We walked through the empty garage and into the spare room,

which was below ground level but comfortable. A big window, with a view that was nearly hidden by the base of an old holly bush, let in the only natural light. The room was furnished with a twin bed, a rocking chair, and a small table with a microwave, positioned beneath a 1970s-vintage hanging lamp. A circular rag rug was the brightest accent. The dark paneling lowered the light below holly-covered-window level. Christine and I exchanged shrugs of *It's not bad—it'll do.*

Lucy led us through the door on the opposite side of the room and up the stairs to her living room.

I said, "Of course, we'll be very careful about locking the door and we'll let everybody know—"

"What do you mean, 'everybody'?" Lucy spun on her heels, wide-eyed with suspicion.

"Oh, it's just that several people will be visiting over the summer months to go with me to surgery and chemotherapy," I explained.

"I see. I'm so sorry. I have a friend who knows someone with cancer. She says she's doing fine now. Another thing, I don't allow access to my living area. The door at the top of the steps will be locked," Lucy said emphatically, taking back the conversation.

"They'll only sleep here, so you won't be disturbed," I promised.

"There was only one time I allowed someone into my living quarters. She was a lovely woman from Guatemala. We got along very well, and I invited her to move upstairs," Lucy elaborated.

We wanted that room, but Christine and I exchanged a glance that said, *Do we need to know this?* Lucy agreed we could have the room for the summer, under the conditions she'd explained. I gave her a check to cover the month of May, she gave me a key, and the deal was sealed.

§☎   ☎§

With dinner prepared, Christine and I settled in and enjoyed a glass of wine while we waited for Ed to arrive. He and I had agreed early on that we would maintain separate addresses. It took the pressure off my mind for sure that I was not on another collision course with matrimony. I'd tried that once and was no good at it. My independent nature held sway, and it was not easy for another to understand how I could indulge in solitary activities for hours on end. Ed had his own reasons, but we shared the cautionary attitude.

This was the first time Christine had met Ed. We feasted on salmon steaks, green beans with mushrooms, and thick slices of Big Boy tomatoes. As we relaxed and chatted, Christine sat back in her chair, crossed her arms over her chest, cocked her head to one side, and looked at Ed through squinty eyes. The presence of a newcomer at the moment of a family crisis provoked suspicion in Christine. I lived quite a distance away from family, and Christine wanted to be sure I wasn't falling prey to a new romance at a vulnerable time in my life. I might give my heart away to Ed, but more suspect was, would I give away my purse?

"What's your line of work, Ed?" she asked.

"I'm safety coordinator for a local produce company."

"Are you from around here?"

"Yes, I was born and raised here. As a matter of fact, I'm living in my boyhood home," Ed offered. "When I was looking for a place to live after my separation, the house came on the market. The timing was rather perfect," he explained.

"Do you have children?" Christine asked him.

"Two. My son is in Philadelphia, and my daughter is local."

"That's nice for you. I hope I meet her on one of my visits."

"I'm sure you will. I think it's wonderful that you can be here for Jane."

None of us knew exactly what our roles were going to be in this unscripted play. Awkward pauses were par for the course.

"Christine and I went to see the room Kate rented," I offered. "It'll be fine, I think. Christine's agreed to stay there tonight and meet up with us in the morning."

Christine neither gave a sign of acknowledgment nor said a

word of agreement. And I missed the signal of her discomfort with the whole arrangement. I was doing a clumsy job of recognizing that I had entered a completely different sphere from my accustomed routine of making decisions without consulting anyone else. I clung to the last vestiges of independence by indulging myself in what I thought would be my last night alone with Ed for a long time. I flung headlong into action naively thinking all was well.

After dinner, I walked Christine out to her car, gave her a big hug goodnight, and went over the directions back to Lucy's place.

Christine's words were measured and firm. "I'm a pleaser, Jane, so I'll go. But sending me to that crazy lady's house is a bit extreme. What do you think I'm going to do? Eavesdrop on you and Ed? You've got a whole suite upstairs."

The damage was done. I'd made a bad start on a very long road of unknowns. *How could I even think of sending my sister away for the night after her long trip and open generosity?* I was weak in the knees with regret.

§☙   ☙§

I woke at the crack of dawn the next day to put the final touches on my revised will. I hadn't made any changes to it since my divorce, and, since I didn't have any legal heirs, this would prevent the state from being in charge of divvying up my meager assets. There was no morbidity connected to this exercise. I was quite pragmatic about tying up any loose ends in the event something untoward happened during surgery.

Christine arrived at 6:15 AM with fresh coffee from the Minit Mart for Ed and herself. I was fasting, so I feasted on the aroma. I took Christine's gesture as her way of saying, "What's done is done—let's move on."

The reason we were reporting to the hospital so early was for a procedure called a sentinel node biopsy, which Dr. Dee hoped would spare me a full underarm node dissection. A dye, or radioisotope, would be injected into the tumor site and begin spreading through the lymph system. The first node the dye comes to is called the sentinel node, which would be removed during surgery and tested immediately for cancer. If that node was clean, another one or two nodes would be removed just to be sure all those affected were removed. If any of those nodes were cancerous, Dr. Dee would continue with a full underarm node dissection to ensure that all of the affected nodes were removed. The thinking behind this procedure is that, if the cancer is moving through the body, the injected dye will follow that same path and will begin with that first node. During the two hours required for the dye to spread throughout my lymphatic system, we waited in our assigned cubbyhole with the curtain closed and made hospital-forbidden cell phone calls, which helped diffuse the nerves, fill the time, and ease us into accepting the idea that this was really happening.

During that time I also answered the same questions for the nurse, the surgeon's assistant, and the anesthesiologist: What's your name? What's your date of birth? Why are you here? Who will be with you at home after the surgery? Do you have any allergies? Have you or anyone in your family ever had an unpleasant experience with anesthesia? Do you have any questions?

At first I referred one to the other for the answers. "I already gave that information to the nurse. Can you copy that form?" No dice. Each acknowledged the redundancy but assured me of the importance of gathering the information separately.

Among the many forms to sign, which held every player harmless in the case of unexpected trouble before, during, and after surgery, there was the emergency contact form. In all my years, except for the nine when I was married, Christine had been my primary emergency contact. Now I was single, living alone on the East Coast when most of my family was in the Midwest. Christine was on the East Coast, too, and my closest family member. However, after my diagnosis and with his okay, I had designated Ed as my primary contact. He'd come with me to many appointments, sat waiting during procedures, and lent a second pair of eyes and ears to the flood of terms, times, and explanations.

My first appointment with Dr. Dee was when I'd shyly asked him if I could put his name down as first contact. He was local, and I needed that assurance.

"Of course you can," he'd said, a bit surprised that I felt I had to ask. "I *want* to be the first contact." He'd anchored me here and closed the distance the miles put between family and me. I neither viewed that decision as giving him carte blanche to access my assets or make medical decisions nor presumed that it guaranteed his support under any conditions. I wasn't derailing the value I'd assigned to my family, either. I simply trusted Ed with the cautious optimism that guides a single woman's thoughts when she meets Prince Charming but remembers all the frogs she's kissed.

I sensed a prickling in Christine. Something was needling her.

"Christine," I asked, "what's wrong? Are you anxious, or is something wrong?"

Our curtained cubby was one of ten that hugged the two sides of a long aisle. Eavesdropping on the mumbled conversations coming from neighboring cubbies wouldn't have taken much strain. I was hesitant to broach a topic that went beyond the usual chitchat that filled the gaps of silence when your only duty was to wait.

"Jane," Christine said, "you have everything figured out. How can I help? Where do I belong? I'm not even the first name on the emergency contact form."

I glanced at Ed, silently sitting in the corner chair that was snugged up against the rollaway supply cabinet. With his head down so I couldn't see his expression, he rested his hands on his thighs.

"Christine," I tried to explain, "you *are* on the list, but since you're here and not at home, one call to Ed will find both of you."

The air was tense. I was tense. So were Christine and Ed. But I didn't know any other way to explain what I'd done. I was completely oblivious to Christine's concern that I was handing the farm over to a stranger. I reached out my hand for hers. She mopped her eyes with a tissue and said, "It's just the anxiety, Jane. I don't know Ed, but I know you. I'm here for you."

"I understand, Christine. I do. Ed's not taking your place or anyone else's. He has his own place, and you have your own place. Your same place." I tried to alleviate her doubts. "You're the first one I wanted to be with me for this. Okay?"

"Okay," she said, stifling a sob. "I shouldn't be talking about these things anyway. You're the one who's going through it. I want to do what you want me to do."

"Well, look who's here!" I said, as Dr. Dee appeared at the foot of the gurney. She was dressed in scrubs from head to toe and wearing super-magnifying-lens glasses. Seeing her was strangely comforting—a welcome relief from the tension of the conversation just ended.

"I think I'm supposed to be here," she said. "Are you ready to go?"

"Yes," I said. "One lumpectomy, please. Measure twice, cut once."

"I think I can do that," she said and then turned her attention to Ed and Christine. "I'll see you two after the surgery and give you a report on what I find. It should take a couple of hours, so don't go too far."

The anesthesiologist asked if I had any further questions before she gave me an IV cocktail for the ride down the long hall to the operating room.

"No," I said. "But I want you to be aware that when you intubate me, I have loads of dental work, and I don't want it damaged. My life savings are sunk into my mouth."

"We won't be using the intubation knife, just a flexible plastic tube," she assured me.

"Then I'm ready."

Christine and I exchanged a warm and teary embrace and then Ed leaned in with a hug and said, "Don't worry about us. You come back to me."

§℞   ℞§

I awoke in the recovery room to see the scrub-swathed body and friendly face of the anesthesiologist.

"Jane, Jane, wake up," she was saying. "It's all over."

"Oh, hi," I mumbled. "Feels like I have all my teeth. Thanks."

"How are you feeling?" she asked.

"Okay. I'm okay," I answered.

"I'll let the recovery room nurse know you're awake. Good luck, Jane." She patted my hand and continued her rounds.

The recovery room nurse cheerfully commented that everything went well in surgery and asked, "Would you like some juice or crackers?"

"Could I have a little more pain medication?" I asked.

"Well, you can't leave recovery until you've had something to eat and drink," she said.

"Then give me that juice and those crackers," I directed, happy to know I could make that decision and speed things up.

I was seated in a recliner in a postoperative room, still wrapped in my hospital blues, when Ed and Christine were ushered in.

"Oh my gosh, you're sitting up. We didn't know what to expect," Christine exclaimed.

"I'm still groggy," I answered, "but I drank the darn juice and ate the darn cracker so I could get out of here."

Ed presented me with three long-stemmed red roses. "I cruised the lobby and cafeteria while you were in surgery," he said. "I got these at the gift shop to represent me and my kids being here for you."

"Thank you," I whispered, hoarse from the intubation tube and still groggy from the anesthesia. "They're beautiful," I mumbled as we exchanged a hug and a kiss. I felt as if I could lean back in the arms of Morpheus and sleep away the day.

"You look wiped out, Jane—but really good for just having had surgery." Christine gave a teary chuckle. "I can see you'll need me as a mediator, because you clearly can't function with all these meds.

Do you know, when you went under the anesthesia, you mumbled something about starfish?"

"Oh, boy," I replied. "I'm teaching even in my sleep. I'm counting on you to get a bead on the discharge rules. I know I can't focus."

"Jane, I called Kate while you were in surgery. I feel much better about the emergency contact form business. She told me that family is first when a medical decision has to be made."

"Okay, good. That settles that," I said, eyes still closed.

"I went all the way to the parking lot to get a clear cell signal," she explained, "and before I knew it, Ed was calling me to say it was all over. I almost missed the post-op meeting with Dr. Dee."

"What did Dr. Dee say about the surgery?" I asked.

"She said everything went very well. She was able to excise the tumor and save the breast. That's really wonderful."

Dr. Dee's assistant came in to go over the post surgical care of wounds and drains. "No shower until the drain is removed in about a week," she began.

"No shower? What do I do in the meantime?" I thought of the ribald song from *A Chorus Line*, "Dance: Ten; Looks: Three." Pits, tits, and ass, otherwise referred to as PTA. "Should I just do PTA?"

"You got it," she answered.

Ed was the only one perplexed at the PTA reference. I guess we gals have our own locker room lingo. Either that or he hadn't seen *A Chorus Line*.

After a short ride in a wheelchair, a twilight tumble into the front seat of Ed's old Buick, and a few miles home, I was utterly exhausted. I walked into the house and headed straight to the first-floor bedroom, where I fell into bed, clothes and all. "Que Sera, Sera" played over and over in my med-fogged head. Doris Day, in her prim suit and pillbox hat, was there, her voice echoing up and through the corners of my mind.

Just as I was falling asleep, I heard the doorbell ring. I counted on Christine and Ed to stave off any visitors. Then I heard the voice of my colleague, Donna.

"I thought Jane was spending the night at the hospital," she said. "This is a sunshine basket of gifts. I was going to leave it on the front stoop, but I saw Ed's car."

"C'mon in, Donna," I called from the bedroom.

"Oh, I'm not going to stay. I just wanted to drop off a sunshine basket."

Despite my stupor, I was moved by her visit and act of kindness. Here was a colleague with offerings of "sunshine" from her, her mother, Kathryne, and two other colleagues, Sandy and Kim. Thin-skinned tears accompanied my hug of thanks.

As Donna left, I heard her say to Christine and Ed, "Now you have to call me and let me know if I can do anything." I had already slipped down on the pillow and was caressing the edge of consciousness.

Christine and Ed divvied up the list of family and friends to call with an update, and I slept like there was no tomorrow, couched in the peace of knowing I could recuperate under the watchful eye of my sister. Tonight she would be safely tucked upstairs in the guest room, away from the lower-level-through-the-garage rented room of crazy Lucy.

§♫   ♫§

Scars and drain tubes aside, my reflection in the mirror showed my left breast unchanged and my right breast with a big dent at twelve o'clock, above the nipple. It amounted to a B cup and an A cup. I was sure that, in time, the swelling would go down and the scars would diminish—I was quite smug about getting away with a lumpectomy and unconcerned about the bruise on my ego.

Christine and I spent Saturday morning on the back porch opening every single individually wrapped gift in the sunshine basket, despite the tag that read, "When you need a little sunshine, open a present." *That would be now, and I'll take all I can get*, I thought.

+ Homemade soup with bread from Donna's mom, Kathryne, along with a goldfish plant and yummy treats from Funk's Farm Market and Garden Center.
+ Karen Rossi angel dressed in pink netting, bejeweled with wire and bead earrings, a chain with a pink ribbon pendant, and a little charm bracelet that reads, "Fight breast cancer." Sandy found her in the synagogue gift shop.
+ Small pillow embroidered with the words "Cats are little women in fur coats." Cat's Meow note cards, ceramic black and white cat that holds a pot scrubber in its back, and a refrigerator magnet that reads "Attention: Chat Lunatique." Donna lives with three self-willed cats, and her hand was clear in the choosing of these gifts.
+ Vanilla-scented candle from Kim, along with the Spring Rain scrub cream and night gloves
+ Silvestri ceramic hanging sign that reads "Follow your heart."
+ Two French dried lavender flower sachets
+ Enya's *Paint the Sky With Stars* CD
+ Two framed ink etchings of flowers by Sandy
+ Metal sign that reads "Of course I don't look busy—I did it right the first time."
+ Copies of *People* and *Architectural Digest* magazines
+ Deck of Hoyle playing cards

The gifts reminded me of my quirks and hobbies, of me as Jane and not as cancer patient, and of what wonderful friends I had. They showered us with casseroles, grilled veggies, and the all-time favorite, according to Ed, homemade macaroni and cheese, courtesy of Judy, my colleague and department chair.

§♞ ♞§

The visiting nurse came Sunday morning and gave me the once-over. "You're doing great with the drain. Your blood pressure is 124/84, and the incision is clean. You can take a couple of Tylenol for any pain you have." She exchanged a bit of medical lingo with my sister, and I could see that Christine was in her element.

Shortly after the visiting nurse left, Christine said, "Jane, you're doing so well, you really don't need me here. I think I'll go on home."

I was more than a little surprised and shaken by this. "Christine, please don't leave because she said I'm doing well with the drain." I quickly wiped away my tears of confusion with the balled-up tissue in my left hand.

"Now, Jane, sit down here." She led me to the sofa and gently held my right hand in hers. "I think you're really doing fine. And I'm not leaving because I don't feel needed. I'll be back again when chemo starts."

"But it's a day early," I pleaded.

"You'll be fine." She smiled and gave my hand a little squeeze. "Now, I've got a long drive ahead of me, so I think I'll get started. I'll call you tonight when I get home."

I felt adrift in the silence of the house.

Ed wouldn't be back until evening. He couldn't have known that Christine would change her plans.

"My sister had to get back home to work," I told the nurse the next day. She was surprised to see I was on my own, but I made light of it. "I have a wonderful support system, and I won't be alone in the evenings." I felt thin-skinned as I choked back the woe-is-me tears.

My copy of the visiting nurse's notes showed that she'd written, "Patient with good support system. Coping well."

Chapter Four

Elective Mastectomy—Not This Kid

Tuesday, May 11, 2004—Wednesday, May 12, 2004

"I got away with a lumpectomy?"

"Yes, you did," Dr. Dee said matter-of-factly.

"No more surgery?" I asked.

"No more surgery," she said. The slow shake of her head signaled trouble to me.

I looked over at Ed and could see that he, too, was perplexed.

"What then?" I asked. "If no more surgery, how bad could it be?"

"Your tumor was five centimeters, and nine out of the twenty-two lymph nodes removed were affected. This is stage IIIA, with lymph involvement and the presence of squamous cell carcinoma. There is no sign of metastasis. The margins are clear, though narrower than I'd like them to be against the chest wall where the tumor was resting. This calls for a treatment prescription as aggressive as the disease."

In breast cancer, staging is determined by the size of the tumor, the involvement of lymph nodes, and evidence of metastasis (or spread) to parts of the body beyond the breast and underarm lymph nodes. If the cancer hops a ride on the lymphatic system, the bad cells can go wherever the blood goes—to all the major organs and the bones, for example. This creates a route for distant metastasis, that is, the same disease can take up residence in areas of the body distant from the tumor. Though the cancer had spread to the lymph nodes, those nodes were in the underarm area on the same side as the affected breast. There had been no spread to major organs or the bones.

The seriousness escaped me. "What exactly is indicated by the presence of squamous cells?" I asked.

"Well, if I were in medical school and given a slide with this specimen to analyze, and if I were told the specimen was from a breast cancer tumor, I'd say 'what is this?'" she explained. "The presence of squamous cells would confuse me. Those cells don't belong there. Squamous cells are present in the upper layer of the skin, not in breast tissue." This echoed the surprise Christine had expressed when I read the pathology report to her.

"How much trouble am I in?" I asked, wanting to be clear about the implications of what she was saying.

Dr. Dee elaborated. "This is a very aggressive cancer. The prognosis would be more threatening, however, if it were showing up in another part of your body. As you know, all of the preoperative tests were negative for metastasis. The probable prescription will be six months of chemotherapy and three months of radiation."

"Do you mean I won't be going back to teaching in the fall?" I asked, ignoring her warnings of how fast the cancer was moving.

Her arched eyebrows betrayed her disbelief at having to spell this out for me. "I encourage patients with equally good insurance coverage to take the time off. It will be your hell year."

Nothing about surgery or chemo scared me. My optimism was grounded in the survival statistics, and I believed I wasn't being asked to endure anything I couldn't handle. I was more concerned about my plans to apply for a promotion in the fall, and to do that, I had to be back at the university, if only part time. I couldn't imagine I would be considered for the promotion if my presence weren't apparent. I had a strong record of scholarship and my teaching evaluations were excellent. I had a record of service that included coordinating projects directly connected to the university's maintaining accreditation for their teacher education program. All of these accomplishments contributed to a high profile at the university. I fought the notion of waiting another year. I was chasing an illusion, letting my success be defined by the moving target of expectations set by others.

"You'll need about three or four weeks to recover from the lumpectomy before you can begin chemo," Dr. Dee continued. "Arrange to see Dr. Oncologist for the chemo prescription. I also think it's a good idea to get a second opinion on the prescription. I'm sending you to see Dr. Macey at the University of Pennsylvania's Rena Rowan Breast Center. In the meantime, you can get started on your treatments here."

I wondered why the second opinion would be scheduled for a time after chemo had begun, though I didn't mention anything at the time to Dr. Dee. I concluded that my prescription was widely accepted as appropriate for my prognosis and that the second opinion was pro forma.

I approached this appointment with Dr. Oncologist with confidence. Undressed from the waist up, I wore the ever-so-charming paper jacket with wide armholes, sat on the edge of the exam table, and waited. Dr. Oncologist came into the room, this time wearing a stiff, starched white coat. The slow shake of her head was reminiscent of Dr. Dee's reaction to the pathology report.

"Oh, don't be sad," I said. "Surgery was a great success, and now chemo will take care of the rest."

She opened the paper jacket, looked left and right, sighed through her nose, and announced without affect, "By the time you're finished with radiation, you're going to have a mess. I think you should have chemo, a mastectomy, and then radiation."

"Oh my." I was taken aback. "I saw Dr. Dee yesterday, and further surgery was not indicated in the pathology report."

"You may not have to have surgery, but you may want it," she countered.

"I think I'm looking at a negligible difference between the size of my breasts. The scars will heal. I can live with that," I gave her my rationalized view of the situation. *Elective mastectomy? I thought. Not this kid!*

I had come to this second appointment alone thinking there would be a discussion of the chemo prescription and nothing more. My lumpectomy scars were healed sufficiently to face the onslaught of the unforgiving killing spree chemo drugs would bring to sick and healthy cells alike. I listened to her prescription and stared with glistening eyes, but showed no surprise. The staging of my cancer as IIIA was my warning of an aggressive treatment plan, and anyway, this office would not be my crying room.

"If you do nothing," Dr. Oncologist said, "the ten-year disease-free survival rate is 21 percent." She pointed to the intersection of boxes on a chart that cross-referenced size of tumor, number of affected nodes, and age. Her fingers splayed like a spider to cover all the relevant boxes. My eyes sought out the recommended prescription for a five-centimeter tumor, nine out of twenty-two affected nodes, and fifty-nine years of age.

She continued. "If you have Adriamycin and Cytoxan every three weeks times four, the survival rate is 29 percent. If you have Adriamycin and Cytoxan every three weeks times four, followed by Taxol every three weeks times four, the survival rate is 40 percent." She glanced up to see if I was following along and then refocused on the chart.

"What I recommend for you, given the aggressive nature of your cancer, is what is called dose density—Adriamycin and Cytoxan every two weeks times four, followed by Taxol every two weeks times four. A day-after injection of Neulasta will be given to promote the regrowth of white blood cells, making it possible to administer another dose of the chemo drugs in two weeks instead of three weeks. Dose density increases the ten-year disease-free survival rate to greater than 40 percent," she concluded.

"I want the dose density," I said. An accelerated chemo plan was music to my ears. Chemo would be finished in sixteen weeks instead of twenty-four, and I would be back at the university in the fall. The illusion of promotion still egged me on. "Dr. Dee recommended I go ahead and start chemotherapy but also said that I should get a second opinion on the prescription, so I'm going to do that."

"I do believe that's advisable. Let's get started at this end. See the receptionist at the front desk to schedule your first treatment the first or second week of June. I'm not in the office on Mondays and Thursdays, so let's make it for a Friday," she suggested.

I didn't. I walked right by the front desk and dashed to the parking lot and the privacy of my car. I sat cocooned in the front seat in a blur of confusion, staring at the brick retaining wall. Gulping for breath, I scrounged in my bag for the cell phone. *What is Ed's number? 569-0379? No! 569-0347? No!* I closed my eyes to see the number, relied on sensory memory, and let my fingers dance the pattern. Bingo!

"How was the appointment?" he asked.

"There's a lot to say," I said, my voice quivering a bit.

"What do you mean? I thought this was to talk about the chemo prescription. What else did she say?" he urged me on.

"She looked at the lumpectomy scar and said that, by the time I'm finished with radiation, I'd have a mess—and that I should have chemo, then a mastectomy, and then radiation."

"What?"

I couldn't repeat it. I was hypnotized by the shock.

"Where are you now?" Ed asked.

"In the parking lot, just sitting in the car."

"Stay there. I'll be right over."

"I'll be all right in a minute. I can drive home."

"Stay right there."

Ten minutes later, Ed swooped up the ramp in his old Buick, headed past my car to an open space, and backed in, all in one fluid movement. In a blink, he was sitting in the passenger seat, leaning over the center console, hugging me as best as the barricade would allow. I could feel his jaw tense against my cheek, and I sensed the gulping back of emotion that certainly ranged from anger to regret.

"I forgot your phone number."

"I'm sorry I wasn't with you. I had no idea," he whispered.

"How could we have known? This appointment wasn't supposed to be much of anything. I was feeling so good after the visit with Dr. Dee. I told Dr. Oncologist that there was no call for further surgery, and she said I might not have to have it, but I may want it."

"I feel like walking in there and having a little talk with her," he said. "This is no way to—"

"Please don't. It wouldn't make any difference," I assured him.

"Let's get you home," he said.

"I can drive okay."

"No, you can't. Let's just leave the car here, and I'll figure out something later about picking it up." His rational tone was convincing. "Why don't you call Dr. Dee and tell her what happened. I think she's someone you can trust."

"Yeah, I guess I could," I whispered, dabbing my eyes and feeling the force of another wave of tears rising in my throat.

We hugged across the console, and I saw that I'd been wearing my seatbelt this whole time. Wonder where I thought I was going.

When we got home, I left a phone message for Dr. Dee. "I saw Dr. Oncologist today for the chemo prescription. She told me something very distressing, and I'd like to talk to you about it."

Dr. Dee returned my call soon thereafter. "What did she tell you?" she asked me. So I filled her in. "I think that's the way they did things in her previous practice," Dr. Dee said. "She's not quite tuned in to the patients in our town. You don't have to have additional surgery."

Chapter Five

Showered with Comfort—
Siblings Hear the News

Kate's calls to my sisters and brothers reaped rewards of reconnection.

I hadn't been back home to St. Louis in years. I'd left home for college right after high school, and chasing dreams had kept me on the move.

My parents were gone. Mom died from congestive heart failure when she was fifty-eight years old. Daddy died at seventy-three from lung cancer. Losing our parents had been crises that demanded we restore joy to our lives or perish under the weight of grief. My siblings and I had filled our walks down memory lane with tears and songs, food and laughter. That camaraderie was a salve for our sore hearts. But the lure of returning home faded without the anchor of Mom being there in the kitchen or on the front porch reading the bookmobile's latest bestseller. It was my diagnosis that signaled the call to circle the wagons of family ties against an unexpected invasion into our restored stability.

৩🐘 🐘৫

Mary, my oldest sister, was one of the cheerleaders on the sidelines of those basketball games where I was sweating and fending off the Holy Angels' spitfire. Yes, a cheerleader—coordinated everything, including pom-poms. Her yearbook picture shows her in midair, with her legs bent at the knees and pom-poms a-flying from her outstretched arms. She wore the classic cheerleader's uniform: a pleated gold miniskirt and a bulky white sweater with a huge gold "A" and a blue megaphone overlay.

It wasn't surprising that she sent me a boxful of luscious silk and pseudo-silk nightgowns and pajamas. When I tore away the embossed sticker holding the tissue wrapping, layer after layer of slinky jammies poured from the Dillard's box. Mary has a flair for fashion, and I was benefactor of her skillful buying-on-sale eye and taste for Greta Garbo–esque loungewear. The backless pink number with delicate ribbon bows at the bodice assured me that the cancer beast had not compromised my femininity.

Growing up, Mary preferred to be called Queen Red. She's the oldest girl and took charge of our fashion shows and modeling spoofs. When Mom let us play with her wedding dress, we carefully removed the tissue paper from the pouffy sleeves and unfolded the organza to its full length. Mary put the dress on over her play clothes, sat in the middle of the living room floor, and directed Christine and me to arrange the skirt in a circle around her. Then she said, "You may bow to me and call me Queen Red." We did. We wanted our turn wearing the wedding dress.

§ 🐌   🐌 𝔢

Christine was the ace up my sleeve to help me interpret the medical lingo. We're just a year apart and enjoy a close relationship in our adult years. We'd traveled overseas together and had often met halfway between our respective homes to confab over our lives and loves. Each of us had been married, divorced, moved away from home, pursued professional careers, and built up a story box filled with tales of the frogs we'd kissed. She often repeated a story in which she claimed I'd hidden under the bed while she cried over a boyfriend.

"Oh, Jane, you know you did it. I threw myself across the bed and wailed over Jimmy Meyers. Then I heard this little giggle, and you scampered out from under the bed and ran downstairs." The story went the same way every time she told it, and every time she told it, I denied it.

Christine exudes hospitality to one and all and thrives on helping out when she senses distress. She's at her best in a crisis, and she didn't disappoint when I was at my lowest and in the gravest danger.

§♌ ♌§

Celeste is five years younger than I. A sprinkling of freckles across the bridge of her nose underscores her Irish eyes that squint and glint when she flashes a toothy smile, the signature of her hospitality toward humankind. Her face, framed by chin-length dark brown hair, is thinning as she ages.

My diagnosis jolted Celeste out the security of her predictable life—working part time as a certified nurse assistant and coming home to three cats and a husband who reveled in 5-for-$10 pizza deals—and into the screeching background noise of a family disaster. She phoned when she heard the news.

"Hi, Jane, it's Celeste." Her voice quavered with a sad undertone.

"Celeste, hi. How sweet of you to call," I said.

"Well, I just found out about your breast cancer, and I wanted to be sure you knew I was praying for you, you know. I mean it's just horrible news. But you can do it, Jane. You're one of my independent sisters. You can do it."

I chuckled a bit, accepting the compliment, and then we fell into an awkward silence. "Maybe I could bring you up to date on what I know so far," I finally offered.

"Yeah, okay," she whispered. "I'd really like to know. Nobody tells me anything. Really, Jane, I'm always the last one to know anything. People don't realize that, but I am."

"Well, I'll tell you what, then," I proposed, "I'll give you the updates, and you can tell the rest of the St. Louis crowd."

"I could probably do that, but I can't remember things all the time." She shied away from the role of the messenger.

"You could write it down," I suggested.

"Well, we'll see. I'll give it a try. And, Jane, I'm sending you something in the mail. It's a relaxation CD that really helps me when I'm stressed. I thought you might like it so you can put the cancer out of your mind and relax."

"Thanks, Celeste, that's thoughtful."

"Oh, it's nothing really. I just need to surprise you with some gifts to make you think of something nice rather than the horrors of breast cancer. This is the best way I can handle it now."

"Celeste, it's fine. I know this is hard on you, but we'll get through it one hurdle at a time."

"Hurdle. That reminds me. The CD I'm sending has a little turtle attached to it with a ribbon. I know that sounds silly— hurdle rhymes with turtle. You should name your turtle, Jane. Okay? Don't forget to name your turtle," she urged. "I named mine Slick; it stands for slow leaps into comfort keep."

§↷ ↶§

Patti is ten years younger than I and lives on the West Coast, where she teaches special needs children. Kate said that when she told her the news of my diagnosis, Patti said something to the effect, "I wish her well, but I prefer to keep a distance." It's not for me to judge the reason why Patti hadn't any interest in contacting me, but I do wonder.

When Patti was in second grade, she wore a brace. Her hip joint was incompletely formed, and the brace spanned the width of two feet, keeping the weight off her hip. Big, brown oxford shoes were attached to a swivel at each end of the brace, allowing Patti to maneuver. I was in eighth grade and pushed her to school every day in one of those old-timey wheelchairs like the one Roosevelt used. We knew every crack in the sidewalks. Patti carried our schoolbooks and breakfast sandwiches on her lap, and we gabbed our way across Osceola Street and up Michigan Avenue to school. I spat eighth-grade-vocabulary venom down onto the heads of those who dared to make fun of her.

§☙ ☙§

Kate was a scrawny eight-year-old when I left home for college. The family photo taken the day before shows Kate in the front row with the younger kids. She's wearing a tan blouse that was kind of bunched up at the waist of a plaid skirt, with suspenders attached to keep the ensemble together. That tan and plaid caterpillar emerged as quite the butterfly in her professional life: speechwriter, manager, and public defender. Her confidence never wavered in her new role of little sister helping big sister.

Kate was the first to send me books on breast cancer, and she clocked many hours online in an effort to be informed. The first care package from Kate came from a wig boutique. The box was filled with comfy cotton nightcaps, turbans, and colorful headgear of all manner. The pièce de résistance was a wig stand. Fabulous! I named *her* Rebecca. She wears an off-the-shoulder navy blue number with a white polka-dot scarf tied in a bow. Her hair is painted auburn, setting off big blue eyes with enviably long lashes. Ruby red lips and rosy cheeks complete the look.

§☙ ☙§

Donna Grace is the youngest girl of the family. Accustomed to taking orders from older sisters, she wasn't convinced she had anything to offer.

"Jane, my coping strategy was to spread books and articles on breast cancer on the dining room table and try to get some sense of what you're going through. Our family has never had a tragedy. And you know Mom—'Put a little Mercurochrome on it, honey.' This cancer business is out of our league."

"Oh, don't I know it," I said. "I've had quite a few books spread out on my dining room table, too."

"I'm sending you a couple of books, and I don't even know if they're appropriate. The first book is on the spiritual side, but then there's a second one that's lighthearted. I heard the author speak and she was really funny. So, just take what you want from them and skip the rest."

"Thanks. Listen, you can call or write anytime. I'm plugging away one day at a time, and right now I feel good."

"I feel better for talking to you, Jane. I'm not sure what to do from so far away."

"Do what Mom always said to do in a crisis. 'Light a candle.'"

"Boy, don't you wish Mom were here now?" she asked.

"I miss her terribly," was all I could say.

§☙ ☙§

Hearing from my brothers, Jim, Bill, Joe, and Eddie, held poignancy for me. They were a bit fumbly in our conversations. Can you say "breast" to your sister? We'd grown up in a household where privacy and modesty reigned. Talk of "private business" was reserved for one-on-one chats with Mom.

Jim is the eldest. Once a badge-wearing, heat-packing police officer, Jim has mellowed in his retirement. Beyond his phone calls to me expressing his surprise and concern, he sent me the dearest little velvet pouch with blades of grass inside that he'd snipped from his St. Louis front lawn. That metaphoric tether to home gave me pause. The distances separating us siblings spanned the country, from West Coast to Midwest to the Northeast. Those little blades of grass shrank those distances in my mind's eye.

ॐ   ॐ

Bill and Eddie called one summer evening from outside Eddie's St. Louis house.

"Hey, Jane, it's your brother, Bill. I'm over here at Eddie's."

I got a little lump in my throat picturing them sharing the call for emotional support. Bill is an avid birdwatcher who traded in his fishing rod and fireman's uniform for high-powered binoculars. His claim to fame in the world of birding is having spotted the slaty-backed gull, which is described on birdinfo.com as "a common coastal breeding species in northeastern Asia, wintering southward to Japan, Korea, and China." The gull was far off course when Bill spotted it in the Missouri Ozarks. Sue Hubbell mentions Bill in her book *A Country Year*, in which she chronicles her beekeeping and honey production business in the Ozarks and the essays she wrote to keep herself centered the year after her divorce. Bill's gull sighting caused an influx of birdwatchers to invade her quiet little corner of the world. Seems Bill's happy sighting was Hubbell's bane.

"We heard the news about your cancer and thought we'd give you a call," he said.

I briefed him on the status of treatments, and he wished me luck and passed the phone to Eddie.

"Hey, Jane, it's Eddie. So, you have cancer?"

"Yeah, I sure do. Can you believe it?"

"Shit, man. Are you bald-headed?"

"I'm going to be once chemo starts."

"Oh, man."

"It's temporary, Eddie. I'm not worried."

The youngest of all eleven siblings, Eddie was just a kid when Mom died. He lived with Daddy, Kate, and Donna Grace while he finished school and then struck out on his own as a big rig driver. Over the years, he dropped home occasionally between long-distance runs.

"Here's Bill," he said, at a loss for how to continue the conversation.

"He gives it to you quick and dirty," Bill said.

"It's hard to get your mind around it, and Eddie's never been one to mince words," I remarked.

"So," Bill asked, changing the subject, "what are you driving now, Jane?"

"A Saturn."

"Saturn, huh? I'm driving a Cadillac," he said with a hint of braggadocio.

"Well, hoop-de-doo! That's terrific, Bill."

"Did you know I retired?" he asked. "The Caddy was my retirement present to myself." Another long pause. "Well, listen, Jane, you take care. We'll be in touch."

"Thanks, Bill. Thanks for calling."

"Prayin' for ya, Jane."

§ℜ ℜ§

Joe is younger than Bill and older than Eddie. He's a reflective man who keeps his own counsel, preferring to take a backseat to the rousing, competitive air that filled our home throughout our childhood. That quiet, unassuming manner made it all the more surprising that, while serving in Vietnam, Joe was assigned to drive an ammo truck. An ammo truck! He wrote that he was so thrilled when he got his orders for artillery that he carried them around in his wallet.

We exchanged letters throughout his year of service: Joe from Pleiku, one of the theaters of operation during the war, and I from my college dorm room in the idyllic suburb of Clayton, Missouri. His letters described Vietnam as a beautiful country, and the little black-and-white photos that a buddy gave him to send to me attested to the stark beauty of scrubby plains ringed by craggy mountains. In his Christmas 1967 letter to me, Sp/4 J. E. Rudden wrote:

No matter where we are, no matter what we're doing—
our family is close—this Christmas is a special Christmas
because there are more of the family away from the house
than any other time before—

I'd like to think of us always together and trust we'll
always be close—

His call to me in the summer of 2004 was filled with
grandfatherly bragging and genuine hope that I'd weather
this unexpected storm and regain my health.

Chapter *Six*

You Look Maahvelous—Bald Is Temporary

Thursday, May 13, 2004

The day after that upsetting appointment with Dr. Oncologist I called Kate to chat about her upcoming visit at the end of May. I took a minute to fill her in on Dr. Oncologist's proclamation.

"She didn't say that!" Kate said in disbelief.

"Oh, yes she did," I answered.

"Tell me she didn't say that," she pressed.

"No can do. She said it."

"That is horrible, Jane. Just horrible. What are you going to do?" she asked.

"Well, I'd like to change oncologists, but I don't want to run into her in the hallway if I do. It's so exhausting, Kate. Maybe I can just play to her consistencies. Take what I need from her and let the rest go," I suggested.

"Well, if you think you can do that, Jane. I don't know." Kate hesitated.

"What? Just please tell me what you think," I begged.

"This is difficult, Jane," she began. "I have to remember it's your body and not mine. I want to make decisions you aren't making.

For example, I want you to come out here to be treated. You can stay with us. Or go to Philadelphia to the Rena Rowan Breast Center for treatment."

"Why, Kate? I'm completely confident in my surgeon. I admit I'm buckling under when it comes to Dr. Oncologist, but my thinking is cloudy. She threw me for a loop, and I'm a little off my self-confidence game."

"I can't tell you what to do, Jane. I can only tell you what I think I would do. It's too much pressure. You've got enough to deal with." She coasted the conversation to a merciful end. "I'll be in next week, and we can do some wig shopping. You'll be all set before chemo begins."

§♏ ♏₰

Tuesday, May 25, 2004

Kate flew from California to Baltimore/Washington International to be with me for the big wig treasure hunt. The rental car she picked up was equipped with a GPS—relatively cutting edge at the time and fascinating to Kate. She's an intrepid traveler, so navigating from Baltimore to Lancaster presented no great challenge. However, the GPS gave her an additional tool for facing the challenge of negotiating the roads of a new city.

Kate led us on a whirlwind trip that started at the hospital wig boutique.

"My name is Marian. I am a certified wig fitter, and I'm happy to help you choose a flattering cranial prosthesis," she said. She was a petite young woman with blondish hair severely pulled back into a bun. This did not inspire confidence.

Kate sensed a challenge and took charge. She's always reveled in getting her consumer's rights worth. Remember that warped skillet? Plus, she has a head of beautiful brunette hair—thick, shoulder-length, and styled in a blunt cut. I wondered if wig-fitter Marian might be eyeing her for a possible donation.

Kate moved quickly among the displays, selecting a few wigs right off their Styrofoam heads and handing them to Marian, who worked in earnest to fit them on my head.

"You hold the front of the wig against your forehead," Marian began, "and I'll make the proper adjustments."

I wore a skullcap to keep my hair flat against my head, and Marian guided me through the dance of the tabs.

"What are you doing?" I asked. "Would it be easier if I helped?"

"I'm feeling for the tabs that must be positioned behind your ears for a perfect fit," Marian explained as she kept feeling around my neck and ears for those phantom tabs. The scene was like picking up a new pair of glasses and having the fit checked by someone who asks you to turn your head left and right a dozen times, lifting up your hair and skimming his or her fingers around your ears. Creepy!

"Now, hold on to the wig in the front, and I'll adjust it." Marian tugged on the tabs and wiggled the wig left and right, only to have the front of the thing slip down my forehead. She stepped back from the mirror so I could swivel around and check the comings and goings of me in a new 'do.

"Oh dear," I said. "I look like I'm going to Thursday night bingo."

To which Kate added, "Yikes! You look like Mrs. Brockman. Here, try this one. It has a flip." The adorable flip style was called Gwen—frosted, full bangs, and a back flip that bounced as I moved.

"Oh, Kate, I've always wanted hair like this. Let's take it for a walk."

Out we bounced with Marian's blessings, although she looked to be in a bit of a daze.

We squealed like teenagers at the fact that Gwen never lost her shape in the wind.

"I'm not sure Gwen is the best choice, Jane. You've never had hair like this, and it would be way too drastic a change all of a sudden. Let's check back with Marian and then go think this through. Let's not tell her we think the wigs are old-lady, bingo-parlor styles, though." Agreed.

We settled into a booth at Louie's Diner and ordered lunch—burgers, with buns toasted to give every bite a little crunch and piled high with lettuce and tomato, and two sides of hot, greasy fries beside a big glob of cold ketchup. After we'd polished off every last morsel, we borrowed Louie's Yellow Pages to map our next move. We found two beauty shops and one store that claimed an inventory of wigs. We started with the store in the heart of downtown.

The wig and turban display in the window lured us in. Bare wooden floorboards creaked under our steps. In the dim light, I could make out a glass display case of hunting knives, cameras, and CD players off to the right. A man with a wise face and eyes was behind the counter and asked if he could help us.

"Do you have wigs?" I asked.

"Wigs? Yes, wigs. We have. Back of store. I help get down what you want." He directed us to the very back of the store, past the racks of camouflage jackets, an assortment of orange hunting caps, and a section dedicated to the resale of used furniture. A few of the wigs were displayed on the bureaus, but the mother lode was high on a display shelf that wrapped around a corner and stretched back toward the front of the store. Wig stands of white Styrofoam and black plastic sported every style from plaits to weaves, in most colors of the rainbow. The reds were ruby, the blacks ebony, and the silver platinum.

"You've got to feel good, Jane," Kate reminded me. "That hospital wig boutique didn't feel good. They were little-old-lady styles, and you don't want to look like that. But this store clearly appeals to a select clientele."

"Well, I'll just get one of these hobo scarves. It'll be good under a hat," I said.

"Yeah, well, then let's get going," Kate urged. "Let's go see the first beauty shop."

But that place was closed. The second beauty shop was also closed for business, but there was a workshop for stylists going on in the back by the washbowls. The beauty shop owner kindly let us in and gave us a stack of catalogs and brochures and a number of hair swatch wheels to look at while she wrapped up the workshop. This place was a gold mine.

The owner sat with us answering questions as we leafed through the brochures. Some of the wigs were so natural looking that we had a hard time believing they were synthetic. I imagined myself sporting the shorter styles. I was a brunette turning gray, covering up the aging with frosted highlights. *Here's a bright side to chemo,* I thought, *saving a lot of money by having hair-on-a-stand.*

"I have clients who wear this style," the owner said, pointing to a tousled Tina Turner–ish flippy wig.

"Oh, Jane, that's so cute," Kate offered. "I think it'd look great on you."

"Can we borrow a catalog and a hair swatch wheel? I'd like to see if we could get them on the Internet. I promise I'll return these today," Kate proposed.

"No problem," the owner said. "We're open until 7:00 PM."

The choices seemed endless on headcovers.com. The Raquel Welch wigs were fabulous, but unfortunately her face wasn't part of the deal. At my best, I look like my brother Joe when my hair is short, never mind *bald!*

"Let's call the help line to see which color on the hair swatch wheel matches what we're looking at online," Kate suggested. She searched tirelessly, and I was so exhausted that I felt like my body was beginning to pleat like an accordion. We zeroed in on a couple of winners—Gaby, a short bob with heavy blond highlights, and Mason, the Tina Turner–ish flip.

"It's all yours, Kate," I said. "I can't do this another minute."

"Oh, gosh, that's fine. You rest, and I'll talk to the help line and return the hair swatch wheel. Do you have a bottle of wine I can give to the beauty shop owner as a thank-you?"

"Sure, sure. Take whatever you want. Do you need directions?"

"Heck no. I've got a GPS in the rental car!" That's Kate—a stranger in a strange city, negotiating the roadways like a veteran.

With the return of the hair swatch wheel over, Kate skimped on the details when I asked her how everything went. "Oh, okay. I thanked her and gave her the wine."

"Get your hand out of those potato chips and tell me what else?" I urged.

"Well, it's like I was saying to you on the phone, Jane. I've got to keep to my own business."

"Out with it," I prodded.

"Jane, I'm from a big city. There is such a lack of sophistication about breast cancer here. Do you want to know what the owner asked me when I returned the hair swatch wheel?"

"Okay," I said, a little anxious to hear it.

"'Did she have both of them cut off?' That is pure ignorance!" she spat.

My shoulders slumped in disappointment. "It's a scary thing, Kate. People know a couple of things about breast cancer, and they're not always true. She must've heard that breast cancer means double mastectomy." This was not my hometown. Nevertheless, I wanted to think the folks were a bit more sophisticated.

That night, Kate found her GPS way to Lucy's rented room. I told her I'd pick her up the next morning and we'd be on our way for a day of indulgent shopping at the T.J. Maxx store in Lebanon, where the inventory is sublime. I found her outside in the driveway, talking to one of the neighbors. Kate hadn't slept well because of the encroaching mold in the subterranean room. She'd opened the window that looked out at the base of the holly to get some air, but that wasn't enough to counter the stuffiness and closed-in feeling, exacerbated by her allergies.

"Kate, what are you doing outside?" I asked.

"Oh, I was just over at the neighbors to borrow a hair dryer. I forgot to pack mine," she said.

Oh dear, I thought, *Kate's being her socialite self and introducing herself to the neighbors.* Then I saw Lucy coming out of her front door. It looked like trouble to me.

"Hi, Lucy, how are you this morning? This is my sister Kate," I said in hopes of warding off any upset.

"I usually don't talk to my neighbors," she said. "We don't have a friendly relationship. And I would prefer you didn't open the basement window. Security, you know."

Kate apologized, but we both knew that this arrangement was on the skids. Somehow or another, we'd find different lodgings for Kate before the day was out. Since my check to Lucy covered the month of May, there'd be no discussion about a refund, just a rationale of mold that would prevent our using her accommodations any longer. I felt a wave of regret wash over me anew, thinking back to the unnecessary upset I'd caused Christine over this ridiculous room.

§ ~ ~ ¿

I figured I would lose my hair by the end of June, so the Gaby and Mason wigs would arrive in time for the falling of the hair clumps in the shower. Once that started, I'd shave my head. For now, I had a couple of weeks before the first chemo treatment. The entirety of those days stretched out in front of me. I welcomed the peaceful interlude free of tests and began looking at life with a view I'd never had before. Edges were sharper, colors more brilliant, music sweeter, food a feast for the eyes and palate. People going about living fascinated me—a kid on a bike weaving in and out of pedestrian traffic and then jumping the curb to take a shortcut through Burger King; a young mom balancing a toddler on her hip and guiding the grocery cart down the produce aisle while keeping up a running chat with the little one. "Oh, look at the peaches," she said to her child. "Let's get some pretty peaches." And then there was an old gent in a crowded Philadelphia Museum of Art silently reflecting on Manet's *Steamboat Leaving Boulogne.*

My longtime friend and fellow cancer patient, Virginia Jan, echoed my sentiments in her e-mail to me a few months later. Her message was laced with her reckoning with the seriousness of her illness:

> As usual, I got the free *Express* newspaper from the same man who always says, "Yes, ma'am, have a nice day." As usual, I paid 50 cents to the woman at the produce stand for the perfect banana. Ordinarily, I might think, jeez, what a rut. I do these things every morning. But I thought about what a beautiful morning it was, and how much I liked getting that paper and the banana. Damn, Jane, I keep coming back to the same thought—I really hate to give up living.

Virginia Jan wasn't well enough to travel, so she anchored her corner of my cheering section with flowers, cards, and Wonder Woman bracelets.

Chapter Seven

Supersize My Side Order of Antinausea Meds—Chemotherapy Begins

Wednesday, June 9, 2004—Sunday, June 13, 2004

"Hematology-Oncology Physicians, this is Ruth. How may I help you?"

"Good morning. I'd like to schedule my first chemo treatment the first or second week of June," I said.

"Who's your doctor?" she asked.

"Dr. Oncologist. I know she isn't in the office on Thursdays, but that's the best day for me with school. If that means changing doctors, that's fine with me," I cagily suggested.

"Okay, let me see what we have open." I could hear in the background keyboard clicks as Ruth searched the master calendar. "Mmm, no ... no ... he's not here ... he's on vacation ... no. Looks like you'd have to delay your first treatment if you want a Thursday."

I chickened out. *Just do it, Jane,* I told myself. *You don't want to delay the start of chemo.* Comforted by Dr. Dee's support and cautious explanations about Dr. Oncologist's manner, I relaxed. The road ahead was so long and there were no recognizable signposts. I couldn't drag one more thing along in my bag of worries.

"Okay, let's schedule it for Friday," I acquiesced.

"Have you had your MUGA scan?" she asked.

"I'm afraid I don't know what that is. No one mentioned a MUGA scan."

"Well, alls I know is you can't start your chemo without a MUGA scan," she declared.

"I'll call you right back."

Un-bloody-believable! I was going to waltz into the treatment center on the appointed Friday and find out I was one test shy. I called R.N. Nan, who showed surprise that I hadn't been informed, and she helped me schedule the test in time to begin chemo the second week of June. A simple checklist to manage my expectations and guide me through a time line of testing could have avoided this spike in my anxiety.

The MUGA scan (multiple gated acquisition scan) is a noninvasive test that produces a moving image of the heart. This allows an assessment of the left ventricle. The MUGA was developed to minimize the risk of damaging the heart muscle with Adriamycin, one of the first chemo drugs I would receive, and one that has been shown to be toxic to the heart muscle.

Two years ago, I had been diagnosed with borderline cardiac ischemia, a condition in which insufficient oxygenated blood is being pumped into the heart. This news about Adriamycin and the drug's possible effects on the heart braced me for a prospective change in my chemo prescription.

With the MUGA scan came my second round of radioactive medicine, this time technetium-99—different nurse but the same lead-lined box, sculpted Styrofoam bed, and cartoon-like oven mitts. After the injection, I lay on a gurney under a special gamma camera that generated a computer movie of my beating heart. Despite my earlier diagnosis of borderline cardiac ischemia, the MUGA scan showed no evidence of a weakness that could be overpowered by Adriamycin. I was ready to begin chemo.

꿍ᴖ ᴖ꿍

The General Hospital Health Campus Cancer Center is a handsome building at the upper end of a long swooping drive, with a half-circle parking pad at the top bordered by a semicircular brick wall. Two sets of oversized automatic doors are tucked under a peak-roofed porte cochere, beckoning all who seek treatment. The building appears to be severed from the rest of the health campus, but I learned you could squirrel through a lot of passageways to access the other buildings.

Hematology oncology and radiation oncology are specialties of the house—left side of the waiting room, please, for radiation; right side for hematology. I was there for chemo—number one of eight in my series of treatments—and my sister Christine was with me. Knowing that she could help me interpret the medical mumbo jumbo comforted me. Before the treatment, we met with Dr. Oncologist.

"Results of your MUGA scan look good," she said.

That was a relief.

"When I made this appointment," I mentioned, "the receptionist told me that I would have my first treatment."

"Really?" she said in complete surprise. "Oh, I didn't know that. Well, since I'm on call tonight, you can have the treatment. I don't like the idea of a nauseous patient in distress if I'm not on call."

Christine and I exchanged looks of surprise and relief. *Hadn't Dr. Oncologist told me to call the front desk and arrange for my first treatment this week?* My heart fell. All the travel plans were coordinated based on this first treatment.

꿍ᴖ ᴖ꿍

The chemo treatment room was quite cheery, really, if it weren't for the eau de Lysol in the air. There were skylights, hanging plants, snacks, and drinks. The room was ringed with an open horseshoe of recliners, each with its personal IV pole and TV on an extend-o-arm bolted to the wall. I chose a recliner by a corner window and drew the privacy curtain because I didn't want anyone to see me if I gave in to the lord of nausea.

"Has anyone talked to you about the side effects?" Nurse Barb asked.

"No," I said, "but I know I'm going to be bald."

"Here are some brochures you might want to read," she said, handing me a small stack of glossy trifolds that showed smiling patients who were ostensibly going through chemo treatments. The brochures offered a pragmatic time line during which I would experience a reduction in my white blood cell count, diminished energy, and loss of hair. I stuck them in my chemo bag, a miniature brown shopping bag already packed with water, peanut butter crackers, and a crossword. I looked at Christine, raising my eyebrow and pursing my lips.

"What are you going to do? It's only temporary," I said.

She patted my hand and just shook her head. I think she knew something I didn't, but knew, in time, that I would.

Christine studied the movements of the nurses, perhaps curious about the details of what they were doing, but more likely using her preoccupation with them as a shield against the ugly truth that I had breast cancer and there was nothing she could do to change the course I was on. Christine leads with her heart, an attribute invaluable to her success as a nurse and one that qualified her in my heart as a stand-in for Mom.

"I can't punch your illness in the face," she said. "So I'm going to eat a pack of Famous Amos chocolate chips. Want anything?"

I shuddered. "The thought of eating gives me the heebie-jeebies."

My custom-mixed meds, stowed in a drawer at the nurses' station in the middle of the room, were hung in a prescribed sequence from my personal IV pole: First up, Zofran, an antinausea medicine to fight the vomiting that can be caused by chemo. Next, Decadron, an anti-inflammatory medication, also used to counteract vomiting. It made me feel very drowsy. Then, saline, a drink for the veins. This flushing of the veins with saline is like having a taste of sherbet to cleanse the palate between banquet courses. And the last drip, Cytoxan, an anticancer drug that works by interfering with the growth of malignant cells. When the Cytoxan hit my veins, it gave me a lightning-strike headache that intensified over the course of the drip. Nurse Barb slowed the flow to stem the pain.

Though Cytoxan can be used alone, that particular drug is often prescribed in combination with other anticancer medications. For me, that other medication was Adriamycin, which looks like red Jell-O in a huge syringe and is slowly pushed into the IV line to avoid damage to the veins.

Nurse Doris, a veteran who played roving guard for the busy nurses, stepped in for the Adriamycin push. She wore the requisite white slacks and comfy shoes, topped with a pink sweater festooned with flashy bead necklaces that got tangled up with her ID badge and clanked when she bent over. She was a good customer of Max Factor, and her roots confirmed that she hadn't missed a touch-up. Nurse Doris deftly kept the IV line slightly bent to slow the flow into my veins.

"Hair today, gone tomorrow," she joked. I liked her style.

The treatment lasted an hour and a half. Not so bad. When we left, Christine and I were armed with several medications and a stern reminder from the nurses to stay hydrated.

"Don't be surprised if your urine is red," Nurse Barb cautioned. "That's just the Adriamycin flushing through your body."

Charming, I thought. *Red urine.*

When we got home, Christine went upstairs to the guest room to watch the DVD set of *Sex and the City*. Virginia Jan had loaned the set to me with the promise that the antics of these gals would be a great distraction to fill the gruesome hours after chemo when concentration is a fleeting notion. I couldn't concentrate the least bit, so Christine got first dibs.

I sat at the dining room table mystified by the pills. I had four different prescriptions, each with separate dosage instructions: Coumadin to thin the blood, Zofran and Compazine to quell the nausea that kept bubbling up to my throat and threatening to cross the line into vomit-land, and Tylenol to ease the blasting headache.

"Christine, can you help me sort out these meds?" I called.

"Sure," she said, bursting from the room and sailing down the stairs.

We wrote out a timetable that served as my checklist. She stayed with me for a little while, and then I opted for a nap. I tried to stay ahead of the nausea all day and slept fitfully that night, in one-and-a-half-hour cycles.

§∩ ∩§

Since I was following the dose density prescription, I needed the injection of Neulasta the next morning. The drug would encourage the growth of white blood cells, elevating my count in two weeks' time and allowing for the next chemo treatment. Without that injection, a three-week interval had to be maintained between treatments to allow the white cells to regenerate on their own.

The treatment center was closed on Saturday, so the on-call doc at the hospital would give me the injection, and that just happened to be Dr. Oncologist. I had the filled syringe with me from the pharmacy, all three thousand dollars worth. Christine and I found our way to Four-West and met Dr. Oncologist in the hallway.

"Good morning, Doctor. I'm here for the Neulasta injection," I said.

"Oh, that's right. I forgot about that. Let me show you to the treatment room, and I'll be right with you," she said with no acknowledgment of Christine.

The hospital treatment room was darkened for the weekend. In contrast to the health campus treatment room where I'd had my chemo—a place designed with the living in mind—this room was overcrowded. Patient recliners and IV poles were sandwiched between straight-backed chairs for patients' companions. There were neither plants nor snack packs of Famous Amos chocolate chip cookies in sight.

"Any nausea?" Dr. Oncologist asked when she came into the room.

"Not too bad," I answered. "I've been able to drink water and eat saltines and keep them down. It's a lingering feeling, but it hasn't erupted into anything worrisome."

"Good. The first treatment is always iffy. Each patient reacts differently," she explained. She gave me the injection and told me to take care, and off we went.

"You know," offered Christine, "Mom used to give us flat Coke for an upset stomach. Do you have any fountain Coke places around here?"

"There's an old-timey pharmacy in the city, Smith's. They have a soda fountain."

"That'd be a good job for Ed," Christine suggested. "Ask him to get a small bottle of Coke syrup from Smith's."

♨ ♨

That night, Saturday, was a restless one for me, with involuntary body spasms punctuating my sleep. The nausea was faint and kept at bay with Compazine. I awoke early Sunday morning to a gentle nudge from Christine. She stood at the side of the bed, dressed and ready to leave.

"I'm going to head home, Jane. I think you're on a good track here," she said.

"What time is it?" I asked.

"About five thirty. If I leave now, I'll beat the traffic around Richmond and be home before dark."

"Oh, okay," I said groggily. "Thanks for coming, Christine. It was a real comfort."

"You're welcome. I'll be back whenever you need me."

I faced the day alone. When I called Ed and told him that

Christine's plans had changed, we agreed that he would check in on me in the afternoon and then we'd have dinner together. Sunday was a work night, and I assured him I'd be okay by myself.

§♞   ♞§

Determined to find a pattern in the post-treatment cycle of side effects, I faithfully kept notes on the dosages and times and my reactions to every medicine. The first round established a reference point for the coming months and gave me a small measure of control. I believed that, if I could manage my expectations, my feelings of helplessness might be alleviated.

Over the course of the next few days, my appetite improved. Half a biscuit, cold pizza, salad, and baked potato—all found their way to my plate as I grazed through the beginning of the week. My need for pain relief was satisfied with ibuprofen. The high-powered antinausea meds were sickeningly potent. Each, in turn, fell off the daily list as my energy improved. By Thursday, I felt I had ridden the roughest swell of the wave and come up breathing easy.

A field trip to Philadelphia for a second opinion on the chemo prescription rounded out the week and provided a welcome respite from a world that was getting smaller by the day, limited in focus by the beast of cancer and the threat of the disease's attending consequences. The University of Pennsylvania's Rena Rowan Breast Center is in the heart of Philadelphia, roughly an hour and a half from home. Traffic jams doubled the time. Ed and I set out three hours before my appointment, and the closer we got to the city limits, the worse the backups became—miles of stop and go.

I called Dr. Macey's office from the car and gave the receptionist our location. She chuckled sweetly and said, "You're not going to make it, but don't worry."

Dr. Macey's office kept us waiting an hour, so I was pretty calm by the time we all crowded into his little office—nurse, nurse trainee, Ed, Dr. Macey, and me. He assured me that the prescription was appropriate for the staging of my tumor and said that he had seen tumors much bigger than mine—some even the size of a small watermelon.

"How are you handling the chemo?" he asked.

"Well," I said, "I do have discomfort in my shins. It feels like bruises. The bone scan showed shin splints, so it may not be anything more than that."

"That's the Neulasta," he said. "It spreads the bones to make way for the regrowth of white blood cells. You say you have shin splints? Well, when the bone expands, the splints reopen. You can count on the first week being uncomfortable, but that should taper off during the second."

"Just in time for the next treatment," I observed.

He offered a sobering prediction. "When will you begin to feel like yourself again? In about a year."

§♫ ♫§

By the middle of the week, the bone pain was intolerable. I tried cold packs, ibuprofen, and putting mind over matter, but there was no ignoring the constant call of pain that reminded me of breaking my little toe in a strong Maui undercurrent or coming down from an airborne volleyball spike only to twist my ankle on landing.

My lifeline between treatments was the on-call chemo nurse, who, in turn, contacted the on-call doc. He prescribed a mild narcotic for the bone pain—5 milligrams of Vicodin every three to four hours. When Dr. Oncologist heard about this, she said, with an air of disbelief that made me feel at fault, "I've never had a patient on narcotics before."

I thought back to the day in Philadelphia. While Ed and I were in the city, we'd met for lunch with his son, Matt, at a great little corner restaurant not far off Rittenhouse Square. The pain in my shins was faint, and I relieved the pressure by crossing my knees and slanting my legs to the side so that the weight was supported by the big toe of my right foot. The floors were concrete, and putting my feet down flat made the pain worse. We chatted briefly about the visit with Dr. Macey, and Matt offered me a bit of advice. "Don't say 'what if,' but 'if then.'" I took his words to heart.

Jane, I thought, *don't sit and wait for outside forces to act upon you, whining 'what if, what if.' Have a plan. Advocate for yourself. You were right to ask the on-call nurse for help.* Even today, I call on those words. They echo in a whispering mantra—don't say "what if," but "if then"—reminding me to see myself not as the wallflower waiting for someone else to decide when I can dance, but as Sadie Hawkins, stepping up and doing the asking.

Chapter Eight

The Buzz Cut—Chemotherapy #2

Tuesday, June 22, 2004—Sunday, June 27, 2004

Milwaukee Carole, a longtime friend who calls a spade a spade, was next up in the choir of angels to usher me to chemo #2. We had met in the 1980s as sales representatives for a computer training company: her territory was in and around Milwaukee, mine, Washington DC. That was many years ago. Now she manages a teenage son, zeroing in on what counts with razor accuracy. I wanted her in my corner.

She arrived on Tuesday, three days ahead of my second round of chemo, so we could have a cushion of peace. She was scheduled to leave on Sunday afternoon. Dinner at a roadhouse café and a spontaneous "buzz cut" at a local drop-in salon to rid me of my lifeless frosted hair marked the beginning of her visit. The first chemo treatment was all it had taken to strip my hair of all life.

"I want my hair cut just like that," I told the salon gal, pointing at Milwaukee Carole's pixie cut.

"I can do that," the salon gal said. Then she took out her clippers and began the shearing process.

When she was finished, the new image of me reflected in the

mirror was fine, with cute little gray fringies framing my face. The view from the rear, however, revealed a head that didn't look anything like a girl's, in the traditional sense. I wasn't surprised at the judgmental expressions directed at Carole and me at the diner the next morning. Our matching boyish cuts, in a conservative town full of wagging tongues, were grist for the mill.

Our first stop on the day of chemo #2 was with Dr. Radiologist. I'd seen him once for a consultation before surgery to go over the details of radiation treatment. This day's appointment was set up so that he could assess the healing progress of the lumpectomy scar and give me the okay to count on scheduling radiation six weeks after the completion of chemo. While we waited for him in the exam room, I took the chance to show Milwaukee Carole the post lumpectomy me.

"This is what I normally look like," I said to her as I opened the front hook of my bra and flipped aside the left cup. "Now," I said, covering up the left and flipping the right, "this is what the right side looks like after the lumpectomy."

"Wow, that's not bad at all," exclaimed Milwaukee Carole. "You look great."

"Yeah, I'm thrilled. You know the saying, 'Put a sock in it'?" I asked. "Well, that's all I need to even things up."

Dr. Radiologist came into the examination room accompanied by a female nurse. He examined the lumpectomy site and was pleased to see that it had healed well enough to begin chemo, and he felt certain there would be no interruption in the plan to begin radiation six weeks after chemo, barring any unforeseen setbacks. I mentally checked that off my list of possible detours in the road to recovery.

From Dr. Radiologist's office, Milwaukee Carole and I walked over to Express Testing for the pre-chemo blood draw, which proceeded without a hitch. The Mediport Dr. Dee installed at the time of the lumpectomy spat back a blood return on the first try. The Mediport is used to deliver the chemo drugs and spare the veins when there are multiple doses of chemo prescribed. Mine was under the skin beneath my left collarbone, and the long, thin catheter was threaded into a major vein in my chest that led straight to my heart. At the top of the catheter was a round drumhead-like form, a bull's-eye for the needle. You could see the round disc under my skin. I didn't like that at all—a foreign object just as plain as you please looking back at me in the mirror. As efficient as that system was, however, a potential drawback did exist, as I would learn later. But on that particular day, everything was fine.

I wore the same chemo-friendly clothes to that second treatment as I had to the first—black slacks, a black three-quarter-length-sleeve sweater with a V-neck trimmed in white, and black Mary Jane slip-ons. But for the second treatment, I gave the dark, monochromatic getup a punch with a bit of jewelry to make the ordeal more festive.

"You can just bring that little bangle right over here," called a nurse from across the room. Then a cluster of nurses gathered, and a chorus of oohs and aahs rose in swells of admiration for the multicolored, three-row beaded bracelet I was wearing—a gift from my sister Celeste. She knew to ground me in softness and frills to balance my thickening shell of bravery.

Milwaukee Carole is all about jewelry. In the days when we worked together in sales, we celebrated every contract won or lost with gifts of jewelry to ourselves. Milwaukee Carole was in a league all her own. She'd buy the stone and design the setting. I, on the other hand, would go directly to the jewelry store where I had to be buzzed in and where I would push my nose up against the estate jewelry case. Milwaukee Carole approved of the beaded bangle from Celeste, but not of my makeshift chemo bag.

"Is that what you're using to carry your stuff?" she asked, alarmed at the very thought of a paper bag. The bag I was carrying wasn't just *any* paper bag, though, but rather a miniature Brown Bag from Bloomingdale's—brown paper sacking with the all-cap words brown bag stenciled on the sides.

"Oh, this is perfect," I said defensively. "It holds a bottle of water, a pack of peanut butter crackers, a magazine, and my crossword puzzle and pen. I use my medical card and a twenty-dollar bill for bookmarks."

"That'll never do," was all she said.

Right after the chemo #2 treatment, I felt pretty good. I knew the nausea and bone pain were still to come, but I didn't suspect they would be any worse than what I had faced after chemo #1.

The day-after shot of Neulasta was the first order of business Saturday morning. As Milwaukee Carole and I were approaching the ground floor elevators at the hospital, out walked the on-call doc. This time it was one of the senior docs in the practice. I'd seen him in the hallways of the treatment center, but this was the first time I'd had any personal contact with him.

"Hi, Doc," I said. "I'm here for the Neulasta shot."

Total surprise flooded his face. "Oh, uh, do you have the syringe?" he asked.

"Yes, it's right here," I answered, extending the little opaque baggie.

"Let's do it here," he suggested.

Milwaukee Carole and I were both caught off guard but followed him around the corner to an empty hallway. I had a flash of being in an undercover sting, about to see the deal go down. I was rolling up my left sleeve when the doc had a change of mind.

"Guess we'd better do this upstairs," he said. As we rode the elevator up to Four-West, he added, "This will be the first injection I've given since I was an intern. I'm a little out of practice." At the nurse's station, he rifled through the drawers, fishing for an alcohol wipe.

Ready! Aim! Stick!

"Well done," I said. "Perfectly painless."

The injections were always painless. The aftermath was what knocked me to my knees. By Sunday morning, I was fighting nausea and sitting up in bed, trying to stay stone still.

"Jane, where will we find the phone numbers for the doctors?" Ed asked. He and Milwaukee Carole were heads-together whispering about what steps to take to find me some relief before Carole went home that afternoon. I felt terribly queasy and wasn't drinking enough to stay hydrated. Any movement of my head started a shower of blinking spots before my eyes and generated a bilious bubbling in my stomach that threatened to rise above the throat level. I shivered with goose bumps at the thought of vomiting. I told Ed where to find the numbers, and Milwaukee Carole took over from there.

"Yes, this is Milwaukee Carole. I'm calling on behalf of Jane. She had a second chemo treatment on Friday, and she isn't doing well this morning. Please have the on-call doctor call me back," she directed the answering service.

It was only a matter of minutes before the on-call doc called back. Milwaukee Carole took the call.

"This is Doc. How can I help?" asked the elevator hallway Neulasta doc.

"Hello, Doc. I was with Jane on Saturday when we came to the hospital for the next-day shot. She isn't doing well this morning. I want you to talk with her." Carole handed me the phone.

"Hello, Doc," I whispered. "I'm so queasy I can't drink enough to stay hydrated, and that's giving me a splitting headache. The taste of water is repulsive."

"See if you can cut the water with a flavored drink to make it more palatable. Take 400 milligrams of ibuprofen now and 200 milligrams every four hours as needed. Try to keep drinking. Continue the Vicodin at the recommended dosage."

"Okay. Thanks, Doc. Thanks for calling back."

Milwaukee Carole sat on the side of my bed for a few minutes. "You have a cozy place to recover, Jane. I'll picture you snuggled in with your faithful feline. And I'll call just as soon I get home to check on you."

༄ ༅

Monday, June 28, 2004—Thursday, July 1, 2004

After Milwaukee Carole left, I slept most of the day and had little luck getting liquids into my body. The water fought gravity as I swallowed. I had to push the liquid back down repeatedly until the regurgitation reflex subsided and the water stayed down.

By six o'clock Monday evening, I was on the phone again with the on-call doc. "I'm taking 800 milligrams of ibuprofen every three or four hours," I told him.

"That's too much. I'll call in a script for oxycodone. It may cause some constipation and drowsiness, but it will help manage the bone pain," he said.

"How long can I expect this to last?" I asked with my eyes squeezed shut against the pain.

"Around midweek the pain should lessen," he estimated. That was forty-eight hours away. *I could ask Ed to pick up the prescription on his way home and take the first dose tonight.* That's what I did.

Wednesday morning didn't bring any relief from the bone pain. I took another dose right on the dot of the four-hour time frame but didn't sense any relief by noon, so I tried to contact the cancer center for help. I wanted to be sure that Dr. Oncologist knew I was prescribed the oxycodone. Her reaction to the Vicodin was bad enough. I thought, *wait until she hears about this.* I cradled my head in my hand, dialing and redialing the cancer center for help. The response time was appalling. From noon until one o'clock, the phones went to a recording announcing that the office was closed for lunch. *Have these people lost sight of the nature of their business?* I wondered. *It's as if they're saying "All patients, please put a bookmark in your pain from noon until one o'clock. Our staff of many takes their lunch at the same time."*

When I finally did reach someone, the suggested solutions for the bone pain ranged from wrapping my legs in warm towels to taking large doses of ibuprofen. Dr. Oncologist was conveying these recommendations through the nurses, and I was incredulous at her not being more concerned. Over the course of the two weeks following chemo #2, I called multiple times, sometimes after hours, and was put through to the on-call doc. All but one of them maintained a noncommittal disposition. I suppose that's because I wasn't their patient.

The one exception encouraged me to come into the hospital for pain management. He was very direct. "I can't help you over the phone," he said. "You must come to the hospital." It's hard to criticize that blast of forthrightness because he was the first person I'd spoken with who seemed to have any sense about the urgency.

I was alone at home without a ride to the hospital, but I decided I would wait for Ed to get off work rather than call him and interrupt his day. The on-call doc took my predicament to heart and amended the dosage of the narcotic. He said if I didn't feel any relief by morning, I should come in for pain management.

Ed stayed with me that night, ready to spring up at six in the morning and drive me to the hospital. I had dusted the furniture, straightened the stacks of papers on the dining room table, and packed an overnight bag in preparation for the next morning's trek. These little housekeeping distractions hadn't bothered me before, but the idea of leaving the house in a mess embarrassed me. What if I didn't return home? Others would find out about the dust bunnies.

That night must have been on the cusp of bone splitting and bone mending because Thursday morning I was able to walk without discomfort. What an immense relief! It was a miracle in my book. But I hadn't seen the last of the bone pain, and Dr. Oncologist would be challenged to come up with a Plan B, since her Plan A was clearly not working for me.

§♪   ♪§

My buzzed hair had begun to fall out in handfuls. The shower drain cover had become shrouded by clumps, and I knew I'd better drop the pretense of real hair and transition to a wig. Annie, my hairdresser, gave me the gift of an in-home shave. I sat out on the back porch and told Annie to let the ceiling fan blow away the stubble. We gathered the big clumps into a plastic bag and sprinkled them in the backyard for the birds.

Despite my firm resolve to face the music of having my head shaved, I wasn't ready for the reality. I looked into the mirror when Annie was finished, and I blanched at the sight.

"Jane, you have a beautifully shaped head," Annie remarked.

"You think so? Oh boy, there I am in all my baldness," I muttered, rubbing my hand back and forth over my naked pate.

"And you have a good attitude. You call me if you need anything. Anything at all."

That night, Ed rubbed cooling Noxzema all over my head to calm the red-splotch reaction of my tender scalp to the vibration of the clipper.

Chapter Nine

Take This Port and Shove It—Chemotherapy #3

Thursday, July 8, 2004—Wednesday, July 14, 2004

"Over the river and through the woods," friends and family swooped in like a choir of angels. They partnered with me to soothe my physical pain, but I hadn't the courage to drop my façade of mind over matter and ask for help with the emotional toll this was taking.

A gift from Milwaukee Carole cheered me. About a week after her visit, she sent me a proper chemo bag—multiple zippers and pockets, printed with two huge, furry cats sparkling with sequined accents. What a hoot! I faithfully carried that bag to chemo treatments from then on.

My longtime friend, West Virginia Nancy, was with me for chemo #3. Early Friday morning we headed for the Express Testing Center for my blood draw. I saw the same nurse as before chemos #1 and #2, and both times prior to this, she had drawn my blood through the Mediport without incident. But this third time, there was no blood return.

"What?" I gasped. "What does that mean?"

The nurse advised me to go immediately to the treatment room and get the Mediport line flushed. If they couldn't get a blood return, then they'd have to use my veins to administer the chemo. This was very disappointing. I hated that drum under my skin. If the port wasn't going to be of any use to me, then my logic led me to request that they simply take it out! The chemo nurse flushed the line and gave me hope that, by the time of my treatment in a couple of hours, there should be a blood return from the Mediport. *Okay*, I thought, *that was a quick fix. No need to worry.*

Dr. Oncologist wasn't in the office this Friday, so I saw a different doctor for the pre-chemo visit. He happened to be the elevator hallway Neulasta doc and the same on-call doc who had prescribed the narcotics. I asked him about the possibility of removing the Mediport, but he said he couldn't make that call without Dr. Oncologist's direction. He did, however, suggest that the bone pain might be alleviated by switching from Neulasta to its parent drug, Neupogen, which would be administered every day for two weeks, in 5 micrograms/kilogram per dose. Neulasta, on the other hand, had been administered as a single subcutaneous injection of 6 milligrams once per chemo cycle. I was willing to try anything to calm the spasmodic reactions my bones had to the day-after Neulasta injection.

The news of a different drug helped me get over my snit of disappointment about the Mediport. West Virginia Nancy and I gabbed away the hour-and-a-half treatment session, pausing for my intermittent drowsies brought on by Decadron. Chemo #3 was administered through a vein in my left arm.

Our friendship of over ten years had taken root while I was in graduate school, studying for my M.Ed. She was the only one among all of my professors who had encouraged me to go on for my doctorate. At first, I didn't believe that would be the right path for me, insisting that earning a doctorate would require more money and brains than I had in my inventory. But she had shown me how to navigate my way around the money part and bolstered my confidence about my brains being in ample supply.

Her stories of renting a big old house near the university—with her husband and baby girl, while she was studying—convinced me that temporary poverty did not have to inspire sadness. She was right. I had three fabulous years as a student. I lived on glazed donuts and coffee, wore jeans, T-shirts, and sneakers, was as skinny as a rail, and reveled in the academic setting. Now here we were, many years later, with West Virginia Nancy once again looking out for me.

"I leafed through the book you sent, *Kitchen Table Wisdom*. It's a good one," I said.

"You can open it to any section," she said. "That's what I liked about it. It's a collection of down-to-earth reflections you might hear around a kitchen table: unstilted and spontaneous. You know, like two friends talking."

"It's perfect. For as much as I usually read, I can't seem to focus on any book-length story these days. It's disappointing, but on the physical level, I'm not even tempted because I'm so tired all the time."

"That'll change, Jane. I think once the chemo is over, you'll regain your verve for reading and writing."

"Yeah, that'll be good," I said, unconvinced that I'd ever see a return to the energy I once brought to being intellectually curious.

§∾   ∾§

Chemo always left me in a fog of nausea and hunger. I felt woozy and lightheaded but craved food. After chemo #3, I craved turkey and swiss cheese. West Virginia Nancy made a quick stop at the supermarket on our way home, where we bought several packages of each, which I ate like Fruit Roll-Ups. After the infusion of protein, I felt better immediately.

As soon as we got home, I crawled into bed to conserve energy. I slept two or three hours, bridging the peak of nausea, and awoke with residual bone pain. I hobbled to the kitchen, absent of any energy to speak of, and stood leaning against the back of a chair.

"Do you want something to eat, Jane? What can I get for you? Some scrambled eggs?"

A wave of nauseous hunger swept over me and gave me goose bumps. I answered no thanks and started to walk away. I turned back and asked her how much time she would need to make the eggs and then I fell into tears. I was crying because I resented feeling so feeble.

"I'm sorry," I said, "I'm just having a moment. Guess I went without eating for too long."

"Fixing the eggs will only take a few minutes, and you can have as many moments as you need," she assured me.

Facing my weakened condition wasn't easy. My control of the disease was limited to what I could read and know ahead of the doctors' visits. My otherwise strong body was failing me. Legs that had danced the night away at Teen Town every Sunday night in high school, swum laps at Marquette Park pool, and walked the neighborhood tracks, were not the legs that barely supported me now. The pain, like a smack from a bat, was concentrated in my shins. Intermittent lightning strikes of pain gripped and flared, causing involuntary spasms. I needed two hands on the banister to get up and down steps. I limited the walking I did over a day's time and gently massaged my shins for momentary relief, fighting this migration toward a shadow of my former self.

On Saturday, we made a quick trip to the cancer center for the Neupogen injection. Since a nurse could administer this drug, there was no longer a need to find the on-call doc at the hospital. Once back home, West Virginia Nancy worked at the glass-topped table on the back porch with her laptop and notes, preparing for a presentation she was scheduled to deliver later in the summer. I lounged in the chaise, drifting off to the sounds of summer mowers and squawking jays in the nearby trees. The ceiling fan worked its hardest to keep us cool in the near 100° temperatures. Occasional breakthrough pain bolted me out of my reveries and made me clench onto the arms of the chaise to absorb the shock and ride the wave's swell. Those shared hours of silent companionship helped me further shed my cloak of independence.

Ed worked every other Saturday, so we saw him for supper that night. He and West Virginia Nancy had takeout crab cake platters from the Chesapeake Crab House, and I feasted on red Jell-O and cubed watermelon. The watermelon served as a surefire way of staying hydrated. The Jell-O took an easy slide down my throat and gave me the sense that I was having a sweet treat. I'd often have a Popsicle chaser just before bed or a little cup of diced fruit. These were feasts for me.

We chatted about the bone pain situation, and I promised I would call the cancer center on Monday until I got through to Dr. Oncologist. I was determined to suggest to her, even insist, that my chemo schedule be changed to every three weeks and let the white cells recoup on their own. Dr. Oncologist would hear the whole story—the abject pain, the inability to function, the unsteadiness when walking, and the blinding discomfort.

Sunday was another lounging day on the back porch. I fought against the tide of pain by doubling up on the ibuprofen, afraid to tinker with the narcotic dosage. I had to hold out until I could see Dr. Oncologist. Between naps and chats, I feasted on watermelon and tried to focus on the *Sunday New York Times* crossword.

West Virginia Nancy started her drive home in the afternoon.

§๑ ๑§

The hope that lower doses of Neupogen would ease the bone pain was dismissed. The effects of the new drug were the same. The ugly, mind-numbing bone pain reared its head over the weekend and moved in and set up camp.

Monday was consumed with efforts to reach Dr. Oncologist. My initial call was placed at 8:30 AM, but I didn't hear that I wouldn't be taking the Neupogen shot until after 1:00 PM, and even then, that was through the pharmacy. A little later a call came in from the nurse, who said, "Dr. Oncologist has finally addressed your bone pain and wants to see you in the office tomorrow." *Eureka!*

Dr. Oncologist had been out of the conversation for the weeks between treatments, with the exception of prescribing Bextra for the pain. Bextra is used for arthritis pain, and the drug gave me a terrible rash. I put myself into the care of the experts, and I was too foggy to think through why there was such a mismatch between my descriptions of symptoms and their solutions. In hindsight, I think the term "bone pain" must have translated as "arthritis," despite the light-up-the-sky bone scan showing my shin splints and the clinical trial results I'd read that reported bone pain in 31 percent of the patients given Neulasta versus the 26 percent given a placebo.

I saw Dr. Oncologist at 9:15 Wednesday morning. "I see that the on-call doc prescribed 20 milligrams of OxyContin every twelve hours and oxycodone for breakthrough pain," Dr. Oncologist read from my chart.

"Yes, the bone pain was intolerable. I needed relief and I couldn't get a hold of you. I talked to the on-call docs." I paused in hopes of a comment, but there was none. "One of the one-call docs prescribed the narcotics and another suggested I check myself into the hospital for pain management. He told me that he could give me a morphine drip to see me through the worst days."

Dr. Oncologist continued making notes in my file, but made no comment.

I paused, swallowing a lump of emotion. I felt certain that she wouldn't welcome soft talk—talk about feelings that couldn't be described with concrete medical terms. My eyes flooded with tears, and I tried to shield my raw nerves, bowing my head and shading my eyes from her view.

"It's as if I'd been hit in the shins with a baseball bat," I whispered.

"I understand. You've been in pain, and this is a natural reaction."

I looked at her through the blur of tears and said, "I missed your voice over these past weeks when I was in trouble."

"Let's take you off Neupogen and change your chemo schedule to every three weeks instead of every two. White cells will regenerate in that time. The difference it will make in the ten-year disease-free survival rate is minimal." She was sober and unapologetic.

My heart was racing with anxiety, yet I couldn't let this opportunity pass to speak my mind. "That's what I want to do. The marginal risk in switching to the three-week regimen is okay with me."

"Have you tried ice?" she asked.

"Yes, ice, warm towels, Bextra—which is for arthritis pain and gave me an allergic reaction—I took all of the advice suggested to me by the nurses."

She nodded.

"If you recall, my bone scan showed shin splints and I repeatedly reminded the nurses of this." I took a deep breath and continued since there was no comment from Dr. Oncologist. "I found it difficult to provoke any sense of urgency from anyone here ..." I'd run out of breath.

"Over the next two weeks, we'll wean you off the narcotics," explained Dr. Oncologist. "We'll allow three weeks before your next chemo treatment and continue with that regimen until treatments are complete."

That was that. The appointment was over. A sense of relief washed over me. I wouldn't miss the narcotics, fondly referred to as the Oxyconcrete Twins for their constipating effects. Along with that sense of relief was the feeling that my distress had been dismissed as imaginary.

Chapter Ten

Smile, You're on Lovenox—Chemotherapy #4

Wednesday, July 21, 2004—Thursday, August 12, 2004

I'd been forced to be the squeaky wheel in order to get the oil, and the change in the chemo schedule from every two weeks to every three had given me a much-improved attitude toward the whole ordeal. I could feel my inner strength against the odds surging back into my veins. Chemo dripped a poison that killed the good with the bad, and I had to pay the price of bone pain. Insisting on relief by going head-to-head with Dr. Oncologist had been the right thing to do.

By late July 2004, only a few weeks remained before the fall semester. I had arranged for accumulated sick leave to pay for my half-time absence. My colleagues had volunteered to cover the classes in the week immediately following chemo, and I lined up experts in the field to speak to my graduate class on specific topics. That arrangement changed the format of the class to one that more closely resembled a seminar—all the more enriching for my students and an opportunity for me to take a breather.

"I just can't trust the chemo beast to give me the strength to teach under those fluorescent lights from 5:30 to 8:30," I explained to them. "It's unnatural anyway. Most people can't follow the plot of *Frasier* by that time of night, and we're asking full-time teachers to get turned on to *Why Johnny Can't Read.*"

My colleagues gave me great peace of mind by masterminding the coverage and dismissing my suggestions that I was creating a lot of trouble for them.

My colleague and friend, Donna, of sunshine basket fame, was with me for chemo #4, pinch-hitting for my sister, Christine, who would arrive on Saturday because professional obligations had prevented her from starting her drive on Thursday. The Friday morning blood draw had the same disappointing result: no blood return. I repeated the routine of having the line flushed, arguing my case with Dr. Oncologist and acquiescing to her resistance to my proposal to remove the port. My veins were the portals for chemo #4.

"Where's the cafeteria, Jane? I could really use a Coke," Donna asked. She'd been on the phone arranging for her car inspection, swapping cars with her son in the half-circle parking pad, and going over my syllabus and the topic I'd wanted her to cover with my graduate class. I sent her off in the direction of the labyrinthine passageways that led to the Fountain of Coke and then drifted in and out of Decadron-drowsiness, relaxed in the knowledge that my colleagues, all aces in the field, were covering my graduate course.

I was raised to never trouble anybody with my picayune troubles, so stepping away to let a friend be a friend was a lesson hard learned. No single one of us could manage the enormity of this beast alone, but each of us could handle a piece or two, and the amalgamation of pieces enabled me to keep life going with some semblance of meaning and mirth.

§℞   ℞§

The continued failed attempts to get a blood return from the Mediport provoked an order for a sonogram of my left shoulder and neck to check for a clot. And sure enough, they found one in there as big as a dime. That meant my blood had to be thinned or risk an embolism of the clot. Dr. Oncologist prescribed Lovenox and continued the Coumadin to thin the blood.

She said, "You can either be admitted to the hospital for the twice daily shots of Lovenox or I can teach you how to give yourself the injections. I once taught a general how to give the shots to his wife. I'm positive I can teach you," she proudly announced.

My eyes widened as I gulped down the possibility of an extended hospital stay.

"Oh my," I said, "even if I could do it myself, I choose not to. And I don't want to be admitted. I'll have to figure something else out." I didn't tell her that I'd given insulin shots twice a day for more than a year to my cat Mercedes. Even so, sticking a needle into my own belly somehow seemed a little scary.

She gave a slight shrug and said, "You'll stay on the Lovenox and Coumadin and have your blood checked every three days until the tests show it's thin enough to prevent an embolism of the clot."

Lovenox is an anticoagulant that helps reduce the risk of developing deep vein thrombosis (DVT) clots. My prescription combined Lovenox with Coumadin to efficiently reduce the tendency of my blood to clot. The injections are given deep under the skin on the belly. The first injection is just below the belly button and then subsequent shots curve out to the right and left like a smiley face. When one row is finished, a second one is begun about an inch below the first.

I understood the problem and Dr. Oncologist's solution, but how was I going to manage the administration of the shots? I called on the nurse wife of one of my colleagues to help me out. The first day's shots were given in her dining room, her two kids nonplussed about what she was doing leaning in toward my belly, which I held out like a spare tire offering. The second day's shots were administered by one of her colleagues, who swooped into my living room like a whirling dervish, asked for the syringe, and plunged that baby straight into my belly. Ouch! Very different from the masterful slide under the skin the first nurse used. From the third day on, the university infirmary nurse administered the Lovenox injections as a faculty courtesy. Turns out that she had been on Lovenox herself and had taught her husband how to give the shots.

Traveling to get the shots was a nuisance, and the tinny taste in my mouth and the queasiness were more than annoying. I'd had so few days of feeling well since the start of chemo, and this wasn't what the books had said was going to happen! I was nauseous, fatigued, and had an acrid taste in my mouth, and I was quickly running out of belly room. The needlepoint track of bruises under my belly button stretched a row and a half already, and I began to think that I'd be better off if my blood was running thick rather than thin, so I could stand up to surgery and have that Mediport yanked out!

As the process of getting the shots unfolded, my right arm began to swell, and the range of motion was diminishing. That made sense since the lymph nodes removed during the lumpectomy were situated in my right armpit area. The absence of the lymph nodes made it difficult for the lymph fluid to flow freely. Edema had set in. Hearing the initial test results was discouraging. My blood was not thinning at all, and until it did, I was in danger of clots forming in the vein that hosted the Mediport catheter. The goal range is between 2.0 and 3.0, and mine was 1.2 on day three and again on day six.

Eventually, the range of motion in my arm improved, and the tenderness of the skin calmed down. Even so, the results showed no change.

Finally, after injection seventeen, on August 12, 2004, my blood count was 2.1. Nine days of Lovenox injections had been required before that number was reached, but I was off Lovenox at last, for the time being, until another recheck of my blood five days later. Based on the August 17 reading of 3.1, Dr. Oncologist tweaked the Coumadin dosage to make up for the absence of

Lovenox and repeated her original declaration: "I'm not removing the port until your treatments are finished."

Even though I still wanted the port taken out, just feeling better helped me cope with her proclamations. The queasiness was gone, the fatigue was not as pronounced, and Dr. Oncologist took time to explain the cycle of fatigue. She sketched a rudimentary horizontal line graph to show this dip and recovery of the white count.

"The first week following a chemo treatment, the white count begins to decline. In the second week, you feel the fatigue of the low count. In the third week, the white count begins to recover. Then it's time for the next treatment."

"Thank you," I said. "This helps manage my expectations."

"Also," she continued, "removing the port would not remove the clot. And then we'd have to start over with the Lovenox to dissolve the clot after surgery."

I got the point. The Mediport and I were destined to remain united as one until the chemo beast and I parted company.

§☙　❧☙

Feeling good after so long was uplifting. I turned my attention to chipping away at getting my promotion application together. This meant gathering documentation of everything academic I claimed I had done over the five years since my previous promotion, along with everything I was doing now and everything I said I would do in the near future. By the time you qualify to apply for full professor, there's a mountain of paper to sort through, letters of recommendation to request, and careful wording of your accomplishments so that a cross-discipline panel can understand the importance of your work. My discipline of literacy education did not translate very easily to the math and science disciplines.

I knew that applying for the promotion was a crapshoot from the onset, and I'd hoped I'd have the strength to update documents and gather them in an organized presentation. I'd made the choice to take the chance. I was going to keep one foot in the academic waters by teaching half time while I finished chemo. My academic record was strong. I was sure my colleagues could rise above any preconceived notions of what cancer could do to a person and see me as their peer versus the cancer patient.

Problems with Mediports, clots, and other technical and biological issues would not turn out to be the only surprises on this journey.

Chapter Eleven

Adios, Chemosabi—The Kindness of Taxol

Friday, August 20, 2004

Kate arrived for chemo #5, the beginning of the end—four treatments to go and no more Cytoxan and Adriamycin. Taxol was the main drip for the final four. Kate had found another place to stay after the Lucy debacle. The university put her in touch with the director of the International Studies program who lived off campus with his family. They often accommodated out-of-town guests for the students, and they welcomed Kate with open arms.

At the Friday morning blood draw, Kate watched while the nurse snapped on rubber gloves, swabbed my Mediport with oversized cotton swabs soaked with yellow disinfectant, and then stuck the needle dead center into the drumhead of the Mediport. No blood return. The port had failed again. After all that Lovenox and the continued Coumadin, I was no better off. Kate said very little but missed nothing. Her face revealed a mixture of alarm and nonchalance, the better to spare me her thoughts as she processed this drama playing out in front of her.

We went right over to the treatment room and the nurse

injected the anticoagulant into the port. Dr. Oncologist walked through the chemo treatment room barely acknowledging me, so I called her over. I wanted her to meet Kate and I was perplexed about the Mediport situation. She moved in so close to me that she stepped on my toes and then directed the nurses to use my veins for the chemo treatment.

"What's going on in terms of the Mediport?" I asked.

"Trouble with Mediports is common. It would not do to remove it during your treatments, as I've explained before." Her tone indicated that this was non-negotiable. Yet I pressed on.

"Why *not?*" I asked. "If I have to use my veins for the treatments, why keep the port in?"

"Right now, the Coumadin is keeping your blood thinned," she explained. "In order to perform surgery to remove the port, we'd have to stop chemo until that reading returned to normal. And then we'd have to thin the blood again to resume chemotherapy." She wandered on through the room without acknowledging Kate or giving me an opening to introduce her.

I acquiesced in silence.

Not until the treatment was finished did the nurse get a blood return from the blasted thing.

Despite my veins being a bulgy map of purple roadways, the nurses took bets on how many sticks would be required to strike a vein strong enough to cope with a three-hour drip. Three sticks and no strikes earned me a ballpoint pen with some drug advertisement printed on the shaft. I won two ballpoints over the four sessions.

With few exceptions, Taxol was remarkably kind to me compared to the first four treatments of Adriamycin/Cytoxan. I had rosy cheeks but no eyebrows or lashes—no body hair to speak of at all. None. The brochure on Taxol minced no words—if you haven't lost your hair yet, just wait. I had one eyebrow hair that hung on for a wiry while. *Give it up, Jane,* I thought. *One hair does not an eyebrow make.* So I finally plucked the lone holdout. I had no discomfort with Taxol beyond constipation and mild med-breath.

Ed stayed with me that night, and Kate found her way to her new digs. We fell asleep watching the Olympics. I awoke around 3:30 AM, restless and overwhelmed by a feeling of helplessness. I felt frantic, trapped. I threw the covers off, jumped out of bed, and walked out to the living room window. I had to focus on something outside the dark bedroom and the needling sensation that I was in a straightjacket. The upset was short-lived but inevitable. All day long I suppressed the emotional toll these little fights against the beast took. Ed said I had to release the valves.

Complicating the issues of coping with physical distress, I was stuck in an "I don't deserve this" phase in my relationship with Ed. I inspected myself too closely and counted the flaws. This was my defense against the possibility that Ed might take me up on my offer for him to scram while the scrammin' was good.

My illness was not a part of the initial package. At this point, I'd been in treatment for the same amount of time we'd been together before the diagnosis. However, Ed is a man who has figured out what's important in life, and he looks beyond the outer wrappings to the heart. He waited patiently for me to trust his commitment.

After three or four restless nights with night sweats and a slight achiness in my knees and ankles, everything settled down, and I had the gift of pain-free days until the next treatment. A mild sleep aid put a stop to interrupted sleep, and that took care of the daytime drags and what I thought was the start of the low white blood count phase of week two. In addition, I had no signs of neuropathy, tingling numbness in fingers and toes, which is a common side effect of Taxol.

I was buoyed by this turn in the tide of pain and charged ahead, convinced I was ready to return to teaching. My spirits and energy were high. I was going to be back in the classroom—my element. On day one of the semester, I had planned to make preliminary remarks about the structure of class, the state of my health, and the confidence I had in my students to reap the benefits of the guest lecturers' advice. I chickened out. When the time came to tell them about my health situation, my thin skin failed me. Someone else would have to tell them. My own news made me cry.

For all the angst and heart-racing anticipation, I weathered my return to school fairly well. Meeting my colleagues in the hallway was the hardest. I think wearing that darned wig might have been what made me feel as if everyone was staring and felt sorry for me. I knew they were only curious and concerned; nevertheless, I squirmed in the spotlight of their attentions.

In the classroom, I looked at my young students and marveled at their hair. I walked up close to them, awed by the knife-sharp parts that revealed a seam of snow-white scalp; by long tresses flowing freely and whipped back into control with the flick of a hand; by natural curl corralled by oversized barrettes and hair bands; by unkempt locks in need of a wash and perking up. All these states of hair were miracles to me. I wondered if I would have hair again, and, if I did, I promised I'd never take that special feature for granted—and that I'd have fun trying out different styles.

When Taxol took my eyebrows and eyelashes, my auburn freckles were more prominent—like a redhead's. Sprinkles of those auburn beauties across my nose and cheekbones called for a change in my wig color. The frosted number I had been wearing, Gaby, made me look like a flat, white board. On a shopping trip with Virginia Jan, we visited the wig shop where she'd bought hers; planning against the day she would lose her hair to chemo. I tried on several in the same style as Gaby before spotting one with close-cropped hair around the face and a short flip of a curl behind the ears. I initially tried the wig on for the style, but I fell for the color—a deep red, with subtle copper and deeper red highlights.

"Cut off the price tag," I said to the shop owner. "I'm wearing it home."

When I showed up for class the next week wearing Nina, my new red wig, my students asked, "Where did you have your hair done? It looks great."

"Oh," I said nonchalantly, "I was with my friend in Virginia over the weekend, and she talked me into it."

Virginia Jan had hoped to be with me for chemo #6, but the debilitating fatigue from her own radiation treatments prevented her from traveling. We played hit-and-miss phone tag over those many months, trying to get together and almost always being stopped by the side effects of our respective therapies. I missed going to brunch at the Old Ebbitt Grille and seeing *The Producers* at the National Theatre in Washington DC, all thanks to the chemo beast.

As Virginia Jan's condition became more guarded, spontaneous calls and visits were our only solace. Ed and I managed to see her for brunch at her home when her parents were in town, and the abiding sadness was reflected in all the faces around the table. Her mom and dad stared into space, trying to absorb the probability of surviving their only child. I wore a silk headscarf because Nina gave me a headache after several hours. I tried to be my old self, but her parents remained sober even when I told our long-standing favorite joke about the cat that peed on the matches.

> It was Christmas Eve and the church was darkened. The choir would intone, "And the angels lit the candles," to signal the young altar boy to come out into the sacristy and light the candles.
> "And the angels lit the candles" … no altar boy.
> (A little louder) "And the angels lit the candles" … no altar boy.
> (Louder) "And the angels lit the candles" …
> The altar boy came out into the sacristy and solemnly intoned, "And the cat peed on the matches."

We all knew how the joke ended and we always laughed. This time there was a smattering of low chuckles from the group.

Ed stood in for Virginia Jan at chemo #6. This was his first time in the chemo treatment room, putting faces to the names

I'd mentioned over the months. We sat in quiet companionship, he reading his paper and magazines on muscle cars, and I doing the crossword puzzle and dozing off now and then. The treatment went smoothly, except, of course, the Mediport failed again, and I was in line to win another ballpoint pen. What a worthless piece of equipment that port turned out to be for me, working for the first two treatments, causing a blood clot and a swollen and sore arm, and leading to all those Lovenox injections and nightly doses of Coumadin.

§Ω Ωᖾ

Friday, September 17, 2004—Thursday, September 30, 2004

Another biopsy.

The results of the follow-up diagnostic mammogram that had been taken between chemo #5 and chemo #6 indicated calcifications at the surgery site. The film showed a nondescript cluster, which meant the radiologist needed magnification views to determine whether or not these little sparkles were fat necroses or ductal carcinoma in situ (DCIS). She suspected fat necrosis calcifications, which sometimes result when an injury to the breast heals, leaving scar tissue that can feel like a lump. The magnification views were indeterminate, so a biopsy was ordered. I had stopped taking Coumadin so that my blood would thicken and make it possible for me to tolerate the biopsy scheduled for the following Monday, September 20, 2004.

I was at Women and Babies Hospital on Friday for a rehearsal session for the biopsy. The radiologist and a technician scurried around the room setting up the equipment. They spoke to each other in a check-and-balance conversation that assured accuracy of the calibration of coordinates for the biopsy.

A second technician coached me on how to position my body.

"Just lie on your stomach and let your right breast hang down through this hole in the table."

"This okay?" I asked, shivering from the cold room and my flung-open gown.

"Here, let me just nudge you higher up toward the end of the table." The technician guided me into place. "That's it, right over the hole. Do you have enough room for your head?"

"Yeah, barely, but it's enough."

"Okay. Now put your left arm down at your side and your right arm up over your head. Just sort of bend it at the elbow and then turn your head to the left." She jostled me back and forth and stepped on the hydraulic lift pedal, and up went the table to a height where she could work from underneath where my right breast hung through the opening in the table. I had the sensation that my body on top of the table was disassociated with the breast under the table. The technician's manipulation of my breast to position it so that the target area was accessible to the biopsy needle involved pulling and stretching, twisting and tugging, the likes of which I thought would result in an additional inch of hang. Gravity was already having its way with me; I didn't fancy encouraging the inevitable by pulling and tugging. These images of fantasy blocked out my reality.

Monday at dawn, I reported to Express Testing to have a final blood draw to make sure the counts were okay for the procedure. By seven o'clock, I had assumed the rehearsed table position. Everything was ready. The technician kindly talked me through each step, reminding me to let her know if I felt any discomfort. The radiologist took her position behind the protective Plexiglas panel and worked the computer controls to guide the needle to the target calcifications and extract the samples.

"We'll start with a local anesthetic to numb the breast," she said. I felt a slight pinprick from the needle—a small price to pay to be numb.

"Now, I'm going to slightly compress the breast in a plastic vise to hold it in position throughout the procedure. It works just like the mammogram compression," she explained.

Several stereotactic pairs of x-ray images were taken. In a stereotactic breast biopsy, a special mammography machine uses ionizing radiation to help guide the radiologist's instruments to the site of the abnormal growth. A very small nick was made in my skin at the site where the biopsy needle was to be inserted. Then the radiologist inserted the needle and moved it to the calcifications using the x-ray and computer generated coordinates. X-ray images were again taken to confirm that the needle tip was squarely within the calcification cluster.

I was awake during the biopsy and had little discomfort beyond that of lying still in a pretzel-twist position for the length of the procedure. I felt some pressure when the biopsy needle was inserted but no pain. I was able to remain still during the whole procedure. As the radiologist took the tissue samples, I heard clicks reminiscent of a toy gun trigger being pulled, much like the sonogram-guided needle biopsy I'd had during the diagnostic stage.

When they had what the radiologist called "viable samples," the session was over. The technician assisted me up and out of my contrived pose and then escorted me back to the dressing room area. As I left, I thanked the radiologist and technicians for coming into the hospital so early to accommodate this procedure. The radiologist told me she would send the findings to Dr. Dee and I would be hearing from her regarding the results. I felt sick to my stomach at the possibility of a mastectomy. Up until now, I had kept a handle on what to expect and when. This was a curveball, and I didn't like it one single bit.

§☙ ❧§

The very next day, I received a call from Dr. Dee.

I was standing in the applesauce aisle of the supermarket when my cell phone rang. Dr. Dee had the pathology report from the biopsy and wanted me to know the results right away.

"The pathology shows that the calcifications are, in fact, ductal carcinoma in situ," she said.

"What's the next step?" I asked, not wanting to hear the answer but putting on a brave phone front.

"I recommend you have a mastectomy once you've recovered from chemo."

"October 22 is my last chemo," I told her.

"Then let's wait five weeks before the surgery."

"Is this really the only option I have? I thought I avoided this possibility with the success of the lumpectomy," I argued.

"Jane, we knew going in that you had a very aggressive cancer."

"What exactly is taken in a mastectomy?" I asked, keeping my voice down when a gentleman shopper cruised the aisle searching for an item written on his list.

"All of the breast tissue," Dr. Dee explained, "right down to the muscle layer that covers the ribs. The skin is sutured back together in a flat line across the area where the breast was. That incision is reopened for the reconstruction."

The stunning reality of her words took my breath away. I mumbled a couple of further questions just to compose myself enough to say thank you, and then I hung up. I felt like I was in a bubble, inside of and yet separated at the same time from the hubbub of shoppers, from my illness, from the world at large—completely isolated and alone though in the midst of a crowd. I considered abandoning my cart and walking out of the store, but I instead went through the robotic motions of checking out.

§♋ ♋§

Despite the finality of the news and recommended next step in Dr. Dee's phone call, I didn't give up on my quest to avoid having a mastectomy. I was sure there had to be another way to treat residual calcifications. The pathology report indicated that this was ductal carcinoma in situ (DCIS), noninvasive and with no sign of metastasis to the lymph nodes or chest wall. I reasoned that, if the calcifications were a part of the original cancer, left behind because the margin against the chest wall was too narrow to cut any deeper, then why not use radiation as the treatment rather than surgery?

I argued this point with Dr. Radiologist over the phone, knowing enough from Internet searches to be semi-informed. He let me make my plea and then deep-sixed the idea, explaining to me the parameters that would make radiation an appropriate treatment for DCIS: clear margins (mine weren't); no residual cells left behind (mine were left behind from the lumpectomy); and no invasive disease (mine was).

"Adequately treating DCIS," he said, "requires vigilance and maximum control of the disease. Your idea is nonstandard and suboptimal." This was disappointing to hear, although I'm sure he could have used words other than "nonstandard" and "suboptimal" that would have been more patient friendly. After all, I was a woman who'd just been told that one of her breasts needed to be removed. If a similar conversation had involved the lopping off of one of his jewels, I feel quite confident that words other than nonstandard and suboptimal would have been used to describe his suggestions for alternative approaches.

I didn't want any more surgery, and I especially didn't want a mastectomy. However, I was out of arguments to prevent that from happening. Surgery was scheduled for the Monday following Thanksgiving.

§✿   ✿§

Friday, October 1, 2004—Friday, October 22, 2004

My last waltz with the chemo beast was in sight—treatments #7 and #8. Milwaukee Carole was with me for treatment #7. I wasn't convinced that she liked my red Nina wig as much as I did, but she kept her comments to herself. I thought the new wig was a kick-ass-sassy little number, and I abandoned the grief of being bald by having some fun with the cranial prosthesis.

I felt less fatigued than usual after treatment #7, and that allowed lots of time to walk, talk, and laugh. This was quite a change from Milwaukee Carole's first visit, when she intervened for me with the on-call doc and took matters into her own hands until someone on the other end of the line paid attention.

Ed and I made a field trip out of taking her back to the airport, driving his 1967 Mustang and taking digital photos to commemorate the event. The littlest things about living thrilled me. Among them, that night, after many weeks of neither energy nor inclination, Ed and I enjoyed a long-awaited evening in each other's arms.

Kate returned for chemo #8, my swan song. Dr. Oncologist was on vacation, and I was glad for that. I wanted my last visit to the chemo treatment room to be a festive occasion, endorsed by those who'd showed warmth toward me. One of the other docs saw me for the pretreatment visit. We had a lively discussion about what happens when a clot forms and how the veins and arteries accommodate the traffic pattern for the blood by forming little beltways around the affected area. Kate sat in the exam room with me, listening in on the dialogue. Later she said that she'd had difficulty following the conversation because of the medical terms that were flying out of my mouth. I just chuckled. Learning those terms had been my main focus and defense against ignorance of my own disease for the last seven months.

I'd brought ice cream and cookies for the nurses. We exchanged hugs and hurrahs, and they awarded me a certificate with a big purple heart for completing chemo.

Chemo #8—over! *Chemo*—over!

Chapter Twelve

The Unfair Flag, Long Does It Wave—The Mastectomy

Monday, October 25, 2004—Thursday, November 25, 2004

I had five weeks to recover from chemo before the mastectomy. This allowed for the recuperation of white cells and time to breathe in treatment-free air. I looked forward to catching up on reading, going to lunch with friends, and lounging my way through life. That was not to be.

I was blindsided by a deep funk that began when I spent the better part of a week feeling insecure and unworthy of Ed's affection. I cried in private and gritted my teeth to keep from crying in public. I had breakthroughs of seeing the beauty of life, but I needed to make a conscious effort to stomp out the demon of low self-confidence. I was sure the dip into depression was a once-and-done event, the cumulative effect of having gone through the trauma of diagnosis and treatment coupled with my repressed anxiety over the mastectomy.

Imagining my body post mastectomy was torturous. I wanted to punch the wall, put my head in the fridge and scream at the top of my lungs, collapse to the floor in a deflated, weeping puddle.

But I kept my feelings to myself in an effort to maintain the same focused approach to this ordeal that I'd held throughout the diagnosis and chemo. I tried to imagine having only one breast by covering up my right breast and turning to see my profile in the mirror to get an idea of what that would look like. In the shower, I covered up my right breast and looked down at myself, again imagining what the view would be like. For a while, I convinced myself that I could handle the loss without causing any alarm to Ed or my family. But I couldn't sustain that conviction. I felt sadness, a sense of "What a shame."

With the mastectomy scheduled for the Monday after Thanksgiving, Kate said, "Jane, you need to be with family right now. Let's celebrate Thanksgiving together rather than my flying in on Sunday to be with you for surgery."

We made plans for her family and Christine to join Ed and me.

One evening in the kitchen, Ed and I were casually discussing the surgery and the logistics of having visitors for the holiday, and I gave in to my fear and horror at the thought of having the mastectomy. I turned away from him to hide my tears.

"What? What did I say?" he asked, obviously thinking that he had done something to upset me. "What is it? Please tell me."

I half-hugged him, giving myself room to rant. I stomped my foot on the floor repeatedly and said, "Why? Why does it have to come to this?" Then I gave in to his embrace and cried the tears I'd been storing up since hearing the pathology results in the applesauce aisle.

"I feel so sorry for you," he said. "You're the one who has to go through it. If this is what has to be done to make you well, then so be it. I need you here with me. You're the brightest corner of my life." And those were words from a man who doesn't throw them away.

By the time the visitors arrived, I was emotionally purged and resigned to the mastectomy as being necessary to my long-term health. The plan was for Kate to stay after the holiday to be with me for the surgery on Monday, and then Christine would return the following weekend to be with me during recovery.

I made favors for the Thanksgiving table from plain brown wine bottle bags tied at their necks with strands of raffia. Inside each bag I put a lottery ticket and a punching-snowman ballpoint pen that I'd found at the dollar store. A local gourmet shop catered the turkey and trimmings, and I supplied the dessert of cherry and apple-cranberry pies from Weaver's Bakery. We were fully satisfied with food, drink, and each other's company. Each of us avoided any talk of what Monday would bring. There would be plenty of time for that after the holiday was over.

"Jane, what did you do with your frosted blond wig?" Kate asked after dinner.

"Gaby? She's tucked away in the drawer. I have a third one, too, which I've never worn. It's called Mason and it looks like Tina Turner's flippy style."

"Oh my gosh," Kate went on, "let's see it. Come on, Christine, let's try on the wigs."

I unpacked Gaby and Mason. I was still sporting Nina because the only hair I could claim were little buds sprouting from my scalp. Christine wore Gaby and Kate wore Mason, each claiming that she looked fabulous. We posed for a picture as the Stair-Steps: Nina was the top step, Gaby the middle, and Mason the bottom.

The men remained noncommittal in their remarks, staying safely away from any opinions, while we three women in wigs raved on about how much better we looked with pretend hair. Kate's son took the opportunity to sneak a third piece of pie.

§♪ ♪₰

Monday, November 29, 2004—Saturday, December 4, 2004

The mastectomy had been scheduled as an in-and-out procedure lasting about an hour and a half. Kate and Ed were with me. As I was wheeled away to the operating room with a little sedation already in my bloodstream, they tell me that I flashed them the peace sign.

My insurance allowed an overnight hospital stay so I wouldn't be alone when the bandages were removed; I took advantage of that benefit. The first day I had no physical discomfort, and the bandages spared me any further emotional trauma. The morning of the second day, the on-call doc would remove the bandages. Before rounds, though, my new roommate was admitted. I affectionately referred to her as Pie Face.

Her first words were, "When I got up this morning, I was looking forward to baking cookies for the gals in the doctor's office. And here I land in the hospital. I was so disappointed." Pie Face lay on her pillow, her features swallowed in a soft frame of fat. Her little eyes peeked out from under swollen lids, with her rosy cheeks prominent and her pursed lips underscoring her ski-jump nose.

"Oh, that's too bad," I said. "I'm sure the gals understand, though."

"Well, it sure was disappointing."

Pie Face told me that she had been living with cancer for many years, and the treatments had been keeping her in remission while frequent visits to the doctor's office kept her on track. The sudden resurgence of the disease had landed her back in the hospital. She was a mopey joe, repeating, with a whiny tone, the story about not being able to bake. When she asked me what I was in for and I told her I'd had a mastectomy the day before, she blanched in disbelief. Her mopes and whines disappeared.

Somehow, that reaction from Pie Face gave me a rush of confidence. *I guess I look okay,* I thought. With that boost to my esteem, I had the guts to face the unveiling of the mastectomy suture.

The on-call doc threw back the curtain that had been drawn between the two beds to afford a little privacy. It was Dr. Surgeon, the same one I'd seen on the day of the diagnostic biopsy back in April. I thought, *Well, well, remember me?*

I asked, "Will you be removing the bandages this morning?"

"No," he answered. "You can remove them. I'll arrange for your discharge."

I was miffed at Dr. Surgeon's dismissal of my possible need for support and an assurance that everything looked fine. Kate hadn't arrived yet, and Pie Face was behind the curtain, so I did remove the bandages on my own. I took a long look at the horizontal suture where my right breast used to be and said to myself, *Well, there you have it.*

§ℜ   ℜℓ

Kate had caught a germy bug on the flight east and had faithfully worn a sterile mask while she was visiting. Despite that effort, when I returned home from the hospital on Wednesday, my compromised immune system had lapped up the germ like nectar. By the time Kate and her family left for the airport on Thursday, I had a vague, scratchy soreness when I swallowed that typically ushers in days of feeling lousy.

Christine arrived on Friday to be with me for the post mastectomy days and she was met with this complication. She and Ed agreed I shouldn't take any chances, and off we went to see my family doctor. I was diagnosed with the beginnings of pneumonia and prescribed a Z-Pak and a cough suppressant with codeine. Christine was confident that the Z-Pak would knock the bug right out of me.

At four o'clock on Saturday morning, Christine was sitting at the foot of my bed, fully clothed and ready to hit the road.

"Jane, I'm going to go on home," she whispered.

"Huh? What time is it?"

"About four. I can beat the traffic and be home by four this afternoon."

"Christine, you just got here."

"That'll give me a day to get ready for work on Monday," she explained.

I thanked her for making the trip and looking out for me. We hugged, she left, and I sank back into a codeine-laced sleep. I spent Saturday in bed, going in and out of sleep to the accompaniment of muffled tones from a *Krazy Kat* cartoon marathon. A quiet room magnified the ringing in my ears and kept me awake. *Krazy Kat* drowned out the ringing.

Ed was at work, his every-other-Saturday shift. He came by to check on me at the end of his workday and found my skin hot to the touch.

"A hundred and three? Where did that come from?" I asked. "I took my temp earlier today, and it was only 99° or 100°."

"Somebody is going to see you. I don't care what it takes," he said as he shuffled through the medical calling cards and found the one for Dr. Oncologist. He explained the situation and was advised to bring me into the emergency room.

We made quite a pair, wandering around as we searched for the ER entrance from inside the garage after we'd parked the car. I was wearing my pajamas and a head wrap and caring very little about the impression I was making. My energy was decreasing rapidly, and a nice hostess volunteer found a wheelchair for me and escorted us to the ER by way of the back hallways. Ed was tense enough to play high C across his shoulders. Kate's bug was creeping up on him, too. He tried to camouflage his sniffles, but his scratchy cough gave him away.

We spent several hours in an ER room off mission control where the doctors and nurses monitored the patients in the bay. Ed hadn't eaten, and we didn't know just when a doctor or nurse would come into the room, so he kept saying he'd wait. If we'd known how long my fever would take to come down, he could've gone to the cafeteria.

Before I saw a doctor, a nurse and a lab technician came in to take my vital signs and draw blood. The nurse started an IV saline drip to keep me hydrated, all the while asking me the routine questions of who, what, when, where, and why. I answered in a small voice, adding that I'd had a mastectomy on Monday. She removed the light bandaging covering the incision to check for infection. I saw Ed put his head in his hands at the sight.

My fever subsided and my temperature returned to normal over the course of four to five hours. It was midnight by the time the doc said I was stable and gave me the option of going home or being admitted for overnight observation. I said, "I guess I can go home." Ed's shoulders sagged. The poor guy was exhausted. I sensed he'd rather I'd opted for the overnight stay, but I couldn't resist the lure of my own bed and bathroom. I'd had quite enough of hospitals. We sat side by side on the edge of the gurney, and I leaned toward him to rest my head on his shoulders. He mistook that move for fainting and reached across me to steady my fall.

We were running on fumes.

Chapter Thirteen

One Is the Loneliest Number—
Radiation Therapy

Tuesday, January 11, 2005—Wednesday, February 2, 2005

"Today we're going to mark the radiation field. You'll have to keep your arm extended above your head for at least an hour and a half. Okay?"

About a month had passed since the mastectomy, and my skin was healed enough to endure the radiation. The range of motion in my right arm was improved to the point where I could raise my hand above my head. Those crawling-fingers-up-a-wall exercises, which I had been doing with diligence, had paid off.

I happily followed all the directions being given and answered all the questions being asked by the two serious-business radiation technologists, and I didn't dare budge from their placement of my arm. That would be the position I'd have to hold for all the radiation treatments, and moving even a smidgen would mean a misaimed beam. Radiation therapy was a part of the treatment prescription from the start because my tumor was five centimeters in size and cancer was found in the underarm lymph nodes. With or without the mastectomy, radiation would have been on the menu, and my calm was grounded in knowing that this would be the final stage of therapy before reconstruction.

Radiation therapy uses high-energy rays or particles, much higher than the typical chest x-ray uses, to destroy cancer cells that might remain in the breast or chest wall following breast conservation surgery or, as in my case, a mastectomy. The level of energy is so high that the measurements are in millions of volts. When the powerful radiation beams strike human tissue, they destroy cell DNA. Cells die as they are trying to divide. Though healthy cells are able to adapt and regenerate, cancerous cells are not. In order for the rays to be guided precisely to the affected area, the technologists take careful measurements to calibrate the angles for aiming the beams and administering the proper dose of radiation. The measurements are marked with pinpoint ink tattoos on the skin to outline the boundaries of the radiation field. A very sharp needle is dipped in indelible ink and then poked into the skin, leaving the tattoo speckle. These precise calculations of field and dosage enable accurate treatments that can gradually shrink and destroy malignant cancer cells.

My prescription called for external beam radiation five days a week until a total of twenty-eight treatments was reached. The tattoo and simulation session was on January 11, 2005; the x-rays to confirm the calculations were taken on January 21; then treatment number one was on January 24. Like a kid waiting for the end of the school year, I counted forward with tally marks on the fridge calendar the remaining days until the whole thing would finally be over.

Each treatment took only a few minutes. All of the time spent calibrating the machine and creating the block to protect the healthy skin had paid off. The long arm of the x-ray machine was positioned so that the lens aimed precisely at the target field. The tattoos marked the boundaries, and the internal blades of the machine conformed to the shape of the block, allowing the beams to hit only the tattooed field. Each step was carefully guided by the technician's input. My boundaries hugged the right chest wall and underarm area, then up and above the collarbone, and back down to the nodes beneath the breastbone in the center of my chest.

The end was in sight. My hopes were sky-high. Before the end of the summer, I'd be sporting a reconstructed breast and turning in my dance card with the beast. But I was caught off guard at my first treatment.

The technician helped me onto the gurney, positioned my arm as we had rehearsed at the tattoo session, and left the room. She took safety from the rays in the control booth and watched me through the two-way mirror. She guided the monstrous machine to rotate to the precise position above the targeted field. I lay there in the company of cold sterility, staring up into the lens, watching the blades configure and reconfigure for each of three separate beam streams—one from directly above, a second from the left side, and a third from below. My reflection in the lens showed me as vulnerable and captive, wearing a pink gown unwrapped to expose my right chest wall and my red wig. I swallowed back the unexpected urge to give in to the sting of tears. *My God, how lonely this is*, I thought. No other heartbeat in the room. No other sound but the whirring of the machine's blades. When the treatment was over, I hid my distress behind a mask of pleasantries and thanked the technician.

"I'll see you tomorrow," I said.

Back in the dressing room, I stared this time at my reflection in the mirror and let my lips quiver and curl through gasps for air to stifle any sounds of whimpering. I pulled myself together long enough to get out of the building and into the car. Dreadfully lonely. Ambushed lonely. One treatment down, twenty-seven to go.

I hid my fragile psyche as best I could, secretly ashamed that I'd come all this way, through knives and needles, only to collapse with the end in view. *This is exhaustion*, I thought. *This is temporary. Right?*

The choir of caregivers caught a break during the months of radiation therapy. I was able to drive myself to the treatments and back, and the side effects of reddened skin and fatigue wouldn't show up until the last few treatments. Each day I put on my mask of contentment and showed up for treatment, focusing on how I would reward myself for getting through the session and the unsettling feeling that I was suspended in time. Those rewards ranged from glazed donuts and coffee to breakfast out with the daily crossword as my companion. These tranquil scenes were thin disguises of my inner turmoil.

Ed made every effort to ease the distress—showing up in the parking lot as I came out of the cancer center to remind me that I wasn't in this alone, suggesting I indulge myself in a little shopping to balance the loneliness, and hiding his feelings of frustration that he couldn't make the whole thing go away.

We took Tai Chi lessons together for a few weeks, saw Roberta Flack in concert, visited Virginia Jan, and went to an Alfred Hitchcock film festival. Oh, and I bought a new car—an all-wheel drive Subaru Baja to get me up and down my steep, snowy driveway and to my daily radiation treatments without missing a beat. Each event was well intended, distracting me a little bit from feeling disconnected. However, I still sat and stared out the window of my house like a little old lady in a nursing home, wondering what the outside world was all about. My usual optimism was repressed. Something inside me had snapped. I'd had enough. *I can't do this anymore*, I kept thinking. Depression and fatigue were my constant companions.

The fatigue that accompanies radiation therapy crept slyly into my consciousness. I was convinced I felt better than ever because, by comparison to the effects of chemo, I was at the top of my game. I noticed, though, that while I was teaching, I would get that sensation of an antihistamine kicking in—that cloudy-headed feeling that sent me searching for words and hoping I could get through the class without my students thinking me the proverbial fool.

My final treatment was the week before spring break, and because fatigue had such a grip on me by then, I used the break to vegetate. Unconsciously, I reached back to a simpler time—that backyard of childhood games and the disputes that Mom would calmly referee. I reached back to Mom, plain and simple.

I'd grown up convinced that I could achieve whatever I pursued. Hurdles were there to be cleared, barricades to be broken through. Mom gave us free rein with our dreams but laced that freedom with the caution that we were not as privileged as others and that an extra measure of fortitude would be necessary to realize success. Opportunities in academics were left up to each of us. Daddy said he'd get us through high school, but as far as college was concerned, we were on our own. Athletic opportunities abounded. Our front hall coat rack was testimony to that—baseball gloves, shin guards, face masks, hockey sticks, ice skates, roller skates, volleyballs and nets, base bags and bats, a pogo stick, and stilts. Somewhere in the box of spikes and sneakers was a pair of pink satin shoes with long silk ribbons, and a pair of black patent leather tap shoes rubbed to a high shine with Vaseline.

Our backyard was an extension of the playing fields at the park. We had poles for the volleyball net, chalk lines for the baseball diamond, a hopscotch grid on the sidewalk, and a rocking lawn chair for Mom, the official referee for netballs, out-of-bounds spikes, and calling safe at the bases. Heated arguments were settled with her calm, "Children, don't fight. It's too hot for a funeral." Siblings and neighbors, who were welcome to stay until the streetlights went on, populated the teams. Then the call would come. "All Ruddens, in for supper!" That was the signal for our friends to run on home. Adrift in a world of onslaughts to my body, I nestled my thoughts back into the comfort of those happy memories—and then more.

A short block away from our house was the corner store. We went there for Mom when she needed the emergency loaf of bread or bottle of milk. Other than that, the store was a great place for penny candy and ice cream. With the little bit of loose change we had in our pockets, we'd pool our resources to cover the cost of a treat. Pennies found on the sidewalk and loose change in the little dish on Mom's dresser made their way into our cash pot.

"Don't open that door so wide, you kids. You're gonna break the spring." Mrs. Yoakum would shuffle out from behind a curtained doorway in the back of the store at the sound of the tinkling bell on the screen door, which we swung wide open to accommodate three of us abreast walking through. A skinny spring stretched to the coil's limits and then slowly compressed to urge the door closed. The penny candy display was straight ahead. The scents of sugar coated everything mixed with licorices and brown paper sacks merged to create a Nirvana for the nose. Whatever change there was from the bread and milk was ours to spend.

"Sorry, Mrs. Yoakum," we would say in unison. She was quick to flip the curtain closed behind her, and we were dying to see what was in that back room. On various trips, we'd spied a kitchen table and chairs and a small television set, and once we saw an old man sitting at the table. He never came out into the store, but we guessed he must have been Mr. Yoakum. We envied him, having all that ice cream and candy just beyond a flimsy curtain—for free!

"Mom wants a loaf of Wonder Bread and a half gallon of milk. How much change will there be?" one of us would ask. We wanted to get the arithmetic out of the way so the divvying up could begin in earnest.

"Let me see whatcha got there." Mrs. Yoakum said, reaching out for the coins and figuring all the math out in her head. "You'll have eight cents left," she said.

With our noses against the display glass and our fingers splayed to keep our balance, we called out the possibilities—licorice sticks, licorice pipes, Sno Caps, Buttons, Mary Janes, Bazooka, Dubble Bubble, licorice hats, BB Bats, Tootsie Rolls, M&M's, Tootsie Pops, Chuckles, root beer barrels, wax lips, candy cigarettes, Slo Pokes, Charms, Life Savers. Those were all within our financial reach. Candy bars were too expensive, and we never would have agreed on one kind to share anyway. With eight cents among three of us, we each spent two cents, then split a two-cent minipack of three Chuckles.

I grew out of the penny candy and ice cream stage and launched into clandestine smoking around seventh or eighth grade. My sister and I blew cigarette smoke out of the upstairs front bedroom window, convinced that Mom couldn't detect the smell. Youth and naiveté make fast friends. In those days, anybody could buy cigarettes. We couldn't leave a trail of evidence, though, or risk Mrs. Yoakum telling Mom we'd been there, so we sent our younger sisters, Kate and Donna Grace. Two little cuties, in their ruffle-hemmed pinafores and Mary Jane shoes, held our coins in their sweaty little fists and swore to secrecy on the promise of a nickel reward.

We sent them to the corner store after a brief rehearsal of how to recognize a pack of Parliaments in the coin-operated machine. If they pulled the wrong handle, we might end up with a brand without filters. We waited in the upstairs bedroom for them to deliver the goods. Their chocolate mustaches confirmed they'd spent their nickel bonus and gave us assurance they wouldn't tell Mom. Parliaments were really neat. At the top of the filter, there was a peace sign configuration of extended cardboard. The cigarettes were long and slender, and that added to the pseudo-elegance of the charade. There was a lot of puffing and blowing through the screens in an effort to perfect our style. I was going for Ann Blyth, with bedroom eyes, looking through a smoke cloud at Van Johnson.

Reaching back to Mom and childhood memories had the unconscious effect of helping me recognize the stuff I'm made of and how I got here from there. That awareness calmed me—gave me the feeling that the essence of my past had accumulated into the essence of my present. The gumption I needed to see this through had been there all the time.

Chapter Fourteen

Inflation Elation—Breast Reconstruction

Monday, April 11, 2005—Monday, May 2, 2005

Wearing a breast prosthetic was an interim measure between radiation and reconstruction. My radiation sunburn healed well with prescription-strength lotion. My final radiation treatment was February 2, 2005. Four weeks later, Dr. Radiologist discharged me from his care. Another twelve weeks were necessary before my skin would be pliable enough to stand up to TRAM flap reconstruction. The TRAM uses the belly flesh, tunneled under the skin, to form a breast at the site of the mastectomy. One of the north-to-south running muscles is also tunneled to support the newly constructed breast.

I made an appointment with a prosthetics company to be fitted, and the session turned into an unexpected debate about just how well endowed I am. For my nickel, I've been a 36B since high school.

"Here, try these on for size," instructed Esther, the breast prosthesis fitter. She gave me a mastectomy bra and a choice of three different gel-filled inserts. The bra was fitted with pockets inside each cup to hold the prosthesis in place. I slipped in the first gel insert, which was flesh-tone and shaped pretty closely to a real breast. The gel filling hugged my chest. A protruding nipple mimicked the real thing.

"You can see the nipple through my sweater," I said to Esther.

"You sure can!" Esther sang and nodded her head in approval.

"To tell you the truth, Esther, that's just not me. I don't care for the look of a rubber nipple showing through my sweater."

"Well, some women like that."

I tried the second gel-filled prosthesis, this one with a subtler nipple. The weight of the gel gave the bra cup just the right form, and gravity took care of matching the hangy-down pendulum look of my left breast. I was surprised at the effect. Esther, a well-endowed woman herself, felt I should try a larger one.

"I think you're a D cup," she said with conviction.

"Oh, I don't think so. I've never been a C, let alone a D."

"But look, it fills up the cup perfectly," Esther countered.

"No, it's just not natural, Esther. It's too big. I'll look out of proportion."

"Well," she acquiesced, "whatever makes you most comfortable. We'll order two of the B cup prosthetics with the flat nipple and two bras. They should be here next week. You can get dressed and meet me at the front desk to take care of the insurance."

ॐ ॐ

The waiting period until the reconstruction surgery stretched over the rest of the spring semester. During spring break, I abandoned my wig and had my hair colored the same red with coppery highlights. I felt fabulous. My strength was returning, I had hair, and the next stop was reconstruction. I walked on air. This was also a time for the choir of caregivers to take a break from the frenzy of medical appointments.

I filled the time with peaceful and restorative activities. Christine and I met for a weekend getaway at the eastern shore,

Ed and I went to the shore once or twice before the summer crowds arrived, and I visited with Virginia Jan before her own regimen of radiation began for a newly discovered spot on her liver. I joined a Qigong (pronounced *chee-kung*) class, which is an ancient Chinese system of exercises that increases Qi (vital energy), bolsters the immune system, and unlocks the body's intrinsic healing ability. Qigong is frequently recommended for breast cancer patients, and I found the low-impact movements and meditative nature perfectly suited to my mental state.

The leader of the Qigong sessions modeled the sequence of movements at the front of the room, reciting the same script at each session. As the movements became second nature, I could be alone with my thoughts in a room full of people. I could wander aimlessly through past events or focus on the future. More specifically, I could focus on what, for me, was the light at the end of my tunnel—reconstruction.

§♊   ♊§

Monday, July 11, 2005—Wednesday, July 20, 2005

I saw Dr. Cosmetics in early June, and he gave his okay for surgery to be scheduled in mid-July. Preoperative tests included a chest x-ray, an EKG, and a blood test. His assistant arranged the logistics. I sat across the desk from her and couldn't help staring at her chest. My word! Her breasts were so full, so high on her chest, and her white T-shirt was so tight. Was this an employee perk? Or maybe she was serving as advertising for the practice—the "sculptors of living beauty." My friends and I teased about my getting "perky boobs," but this gal was in a league all her own.

Christine arrived the night before surgery. She, Ed, and I reported to the hospital at 6:00 AM for a 7:30 slot in the operating room. We waited in another curtained-off nook, making small talk in anticipation of Dr. Cosmetics's arrival. Christine reached into her purse for tissues, and I noticed her teary eyes.

"Christine, are you okay?" I asked.

"Yeah, I just want these in case I cry."

"Please don't cry. This is a *happy* thing. It's the end of the trail, and I'm not worried."

"Okay," she said. "That's a good way to look at it."

The tone lightened just in time for the curtain to swish back and Dr. Cosmetics to make his entrance. We exchanged perfunctory "Good mornings," and I asked if he'd had a good night's sleep.

"I'm fine this morning," he said.

Okay, then. That was the end of small talk.

Dr. Cosmetics had his personal kit of black markers and tape measures to mark the map of reconstruction on my stomach and chest. I stood in front of him, and he lifted my hospital gown up to my neck. There I was in my all-together, with Christine putting her hand up to shade her eyes away and Ed casting his head down, to assure me they were just as surprised by the abrupt unveiling. Dr. Cosmetics measured me from hip to hip, drew a dotted line in the shape of an oval just below my navel, and then measured from that point A to point B, the mastectomy suture line. At point B, he drew a circle with the black marker to outline the target area for the reconstructed breast.

The medical players came into our curtained cubby one at a time to ask their requisite questions—nurse, anesthesiologist, and IV technician. The surgery would last the better part of five hours. After receiving warm hugs and words of "We'll be waiting" from Christine and Ed, my gurney was whooshed out of the nook and down the hall to the OR.

§∩ ∩§

Our hearts were light: the surgery had been a success. Christine and I spent my five days of hospital recovery gabbing and laughing about this and that. One day she brought in a huge bag of candy and three gift bags. She divided the loot into the bags, and we wrote notes of thanks for each of the nursing shifts.

"They'll appreciate this," Christine said. "I remember my days on the floor. We were always nibbling on snacks. It made us feel good when a patient gave us a token of their appreciation." She clearly marked each bag with the shift hours, knowing full well that the first shift to get the bags would likely extend their sweet teeth to the rest of the bounty unless our distribution instructions were specified.

We oohed and aahed at my reconstructed breast, packaged in what appeared to be clear tape. Every few hours, around the clock, a nurse inspected the flap with a pinpoint flashlight, to look for any signs of infection and to chart the healing progress. One night the nurse came in to inspect the site and made a comment that surprised and worried me.

"It seems cold to the touch. I don't think that's as it should be," she said.

My heart fluttered and skipped a beat at the thought of something going wrong. I said nothing at the time but made a mental note to ask Dr. Cosmetics about the nurse's assessment during morning rounds.

"There's nothing going on here that's out of the ordinary," he stated. "It's healing nicely. We'll remove the first two drains before your discharge on Friday, and I'll see you in my office on Monday to remove the last drain."

His words were music to my ears. The drains were removed as promised on Friday morning, and I was dressed and waiting for the discharge papers when Ed's daughter, Chris, dropped in for a visit. Perfect timing. My Christine, Ed's Chris, and I made a tight little trio inspecting the belly turned breast. We joked over that being one way to redistribute the cellulite. Christine got me situated in the wheelchair for the great escape and piled my lap with flowers, cards, and all the hospital goodies, right down to the spit-up pan. Ed's Chris promised a suppertime visit and said she'd even bring the supper—a perfect present.

Home by early afternoon, we were soon installed on the back porch to catch any breeze the July heat might offer. I lounged in the wicker chaise, and Christine sat in a cushioned chair at the glass-topped table. Her half-lens readers were perched on the end of her nose as she thumbed through a magazine. I looked at her with new eyes. Across the many months, I had wondered and worried over her apparent restlessness to leave not long after she'd arrived. Before this trip we'd had a heart-to-heart chat, and I realized that I was completely blind to the effects my illness was having on my loved ones. I had kept my sanity through a determination to understand what was happening inside me, and that point of view had sustained me on a logical and focused path. But I had wrongly assumed that everyone else was viewing the situation the same way. Christine was kind and frank with me as she explained her feelings.

"I need a job to do, Jane. I need to feel useful," she explained. "That's why I'm always offering to clean the bathroom or dust the house." We laughed over that because the first time she suggested those projects, I asked her if she thought my house was dirty.

Our chat led to my clearer understanding of her point of view and, of course, to a list of jobs for her. She cleaned my bathroom from top to bottom, dusted the furniture, and spread twenty-five bags of mulch on a huge flowerbed in the backyard. She worked in one hundred degree temperatures, slitting the plastic mulch bags, laying them as a weed barrier, and spreading the mulch by hand. The job was enormous. The end result was a thick bed of dark brown hardwood mulch embracing the trees. The refreshing fragrance of chipped wood permeated the air and wafted up to the porch, where I inhaled the smell with sighs of satisfaction.

The weekend passed at a slow motion typical of hot summer days. Though I slept well at night, I'd awaken with night sweats and detect a faint odor that I attributed to the sweating. I had an appointment with Dr. Cosmetics on Monday to have the final drain removed. I would tell him then.

At that appointment, he inspected the reconstruction site and noted the redness on my chest. "It might be bruising or possibly an infection. We'll put you on Cipro just in case."

That satisfied Christine and me. Things were under control. If I had developed an infection, Cipro would stop its advancement. We started taking my temperature to track the unlikely presence of an infection. But unlikely swiftly turned into pretty much of a sure thing within twenty-four hours when, on Tuesday, I ran a temperature of 102.5°. Christine called Dr. Cosmetics and was given to the on-call doc. Since I wasn't his patient, he was reluctant to see me. He suggested that Christine either take me to the ER or call the office in the morning for an appointment. His suggestions unsettled Christine because she sensed a need for urgency: I had a fever and was very sluggish, and the smell from the site was getting more pungent. I resisted going to the ER, however, and she honored my wishes, against her better judgment.

First thing Wednesday morning, Christine called for an appointment and was given a 4:30 PM slot.

§℧ ℧ℇ

The wait seemed interminable. My temperature was rising, and I was becoming more restless. As I cradled my head in my left hand, trying to doze off for a few minutes, Christine looked over at me and said, "Get your clothes on, girl. We're going to the ER." I acquiesced without so much as a whimper.

The ER triage nurse took one look at the smelly site and led us into one of several private rooms, all joined by a common back hall that housed the triage medical supplies.

"You can't wait out in the hall with that infection," she explained. Then she sat me in a reclining chair, took my temperature, and tried to make me comfortable. She told us that Dr. Cosmetics was in surgery and was expected to be free in the next half hour.

Christine and I were relieved to be sitting in the lap of medical help. While waiting for Dr. Cosmetics, we entertained ourselves by eavesdropping on the adjoining room. The voices carried easily through the common hallway. A mother had brought her toddler in because she wasn't eating her rice. Christine peeked around the corner and came back into our space giggling. "She's a little pudge ball with the cutest sneakers."

The next was a mom with her little boy who had taken a flying leap for the pool but had missed and landed facedown onto the cement pool deck. Christine's peek revealed a freckle-faced kid marked with fresh vertical scratches from the nubby cement. His mom kept up a running commentary to distract the would-be Olympian diver. "You're such a brave little boy. Everything is going to be fine, honey." She balanced a baby girl on her hip, swaying back and forth, cooing comforting sounds to block any frights a hospital might cause in a little one.

When Dr. Cosmetics finally arrived, he assessed the reconstruction site and said to Christine, "You should have brought her in sooner."

That really scalded me. If anyone was to blame for the delay, it was the on-call doc. If he hadn't been so nonchalant about the matter, I would have already been seen.

"I can't do anything this evening," Dr. Cosmetics went on, "but I'm going to admit you and schedule you for surgery tomorrow. We'll take a close look at the reconstruction site and determine the extent of the infection." No other action was taken that day other than to admit me.

Christine saved my life—no two ways about that. Thanks to her medical alarm going off, sepsis was averted. If we had followed the advice of the on-call doc, taking a late-in-the-day appointment, where would I have been then? But an even more significant question is what if someone had paid attention to that astute nurse who noticed that something wasn't right while I was still in the hospital right after the reconstruction surgery? How much of the grief yet to come might have been prevented?

Chapter Fifteen

Deflation Depression—A Failed Reconstruction

Thursday, July 21, 2005—Wednesday, August 17, 2005

I was admitted and assigned to a room on a floor reserved for brain trauma patients.

There were no rooms available on the floor reserved for cancer patients, and my condition required that I be among nurses who were familiar with traumatic injuries. The room was freezing, a situation made worse by the fact that the bed was located near the heating and cooling vent, which was cooling at a midsummer blast. I shivered under four blankets and had a fifth draped over the vent. We turned the bed so that one side hugged the interior wall, which helped a little. Shortly thereafter, the engineer came to the room and announced there was really nothing he could do because everything was controlled by the master unit on the roof. By the time Ed joined us in the room at the end of his workday, there were nurses asking me admission questions and taking my vital signs, an engineer with a clanking leather tool belt looking for ways to divert the arctic blast, and Christine helping me rearrange the room.

"Jane, you have a raging infection, and here you are rearranging the damn furniture," Christine said, half-laughing.

Thursday morning visitors included Dr. Cosmetics and Dr. Infectious Diseases. Oh my. They took a culture from the suture edge of the reconstruction site. The smelliest of smelly goop came away on the cotton tip of a long swab, which was put into a vial and the top plugged. That evening I was taken to the OR for that "closer look." The gurney was whisked out of the room and down the hall to the melodies of "Good luck" and "See you later" from the nurses.

Christine wasn't feeling at all cheery, and apparently, once I was down the hall and out of sight, she approached the head nurse at the charting station. "My sister is really sick, isn't she?" she told me she'd asked them. She was tearfully pleading for information to help her clearly assess the situation.

"Yes, she is," said the R.N.

"I thought so," was all Christine could say. The line between her heart and her nurse-ness was blurring.

She had assumed the role of medical watchdog, and her confidence returned in a rush when she and Ed met with Dr. Cosmetics immediately after my surgery to get the report. I heard the whole story later. According to Christine, Dr. Cosmetics came into the conference room, sat down, and began by saying, "It's not good news. The infection had gone too far. I had to remove the TRAM flap."

Ed was beside himself. "What are you telling us? How could this happen? Do you know what she's been through already?"

Dr. Cosmetics pushed his chair back and said, "Please, ask me all of your questions." He, too, was beside himself. "This has never happened with any of my other patients," he said.

Christine leaned toward Ed, put her hand on his forearm, and said, "Ed, I don't think you understand what's being said. The infection was headed for her bloodstream. It could have taken her." She was calm and confident; she understood Dr. Cosmetics's decision.

Ed was slightly consoled by that explanation. His emotions ran the gamut of "Why was Jane's reconstruction Dr. Cosmetics's first failure?" to "Thank God she's alive."

"Who's going to tell Jane?" he asked. "I can't do it. Not after all she's been through. She's been looking forward to reconstruction as making her feel whole again. I just don't think I can present this properly."

"Usually, I would tell her," Dr. Cosmetics said, "but I'll be gone by the time she's out of recovery."

Christine volunteered to deliver the news.

Once Dr. Cosmetics left the room, Ed let his frustrations fly. "How can Dr. Cosmetics not take ownership for this? Shouldn't he wait until Jane is out of recovery, or come back later?"

From recovery, I was taken back to my room flanked by the nurses, Christine, and Ed. Relief washed over me to be finished with the surgery, and I rode a wave of renewed hope that everything was okay. Christine was at the foot of the gurney as I was wheeled into my room. Ed told me later that he had stayed back, outside the room, knowing what Christine was about to say to me. He was wracked with emotion and characterized the removal of the flap as "the worst possible turn of events."

"Jane, did they talk to you downstairs?" Christine asked.

"No," I answered.

"He had to remove the flap," she said, holding onto my hand while I was shifted from the gurney to the bed.

"Oh, did he?" I asked, and then, without warning, the rush of emotion rose in my throat. My wailing, "No! No!" echoed out into the hall where Ed stood. In the space of one week's time, he had watched me go from being a reconstruction patient to being a wound patient, with no words of transition.

Christine and I had a cry together, and I whispered to her, "If it was that far gone, I'm glad it's out."

She couldn't speak, but her warmth and concern showed in her eyes and I felt it in her touch. She looked beyond me to the door and said, "It's okay, come on in."

She was speaking to a nurse who'd come to wish me well and to Ed. He was solemn, and I could see his jaw working as he struggled to hold back tears. He held my hand and hugged me, and I assured him I was okay.

He said, "I haven't put away the unfair flag."

§⟋   ⟍₰

My wound was bound with layers of gauze wrapped around my chest to hold the bandaging in place. Dr. Cosmetics changed the bandage the next morning, and I had my first look at the site. I had an open wound on my chest measuring 9.5 × 15.5 × 0.3 centimeters, with a depth of 1.5 centimeters at the three o'clock position. This boundary defined a field of red flesh that looked like raw meat but was actually the muscle covering the ribs, which were clearly visible through the thin muscle layer. Diagnosis—right chest cellulitis—an infection of the deep subcutaneous tissue of the skin, caused by infection with *Staphylococcus, Streptococcus,* or other bacteria, and incidentally, over the nine days I spent in the hospital, *Staphylococcus* was the only thing that grew in the petri dish from the swab taken on my first day there.

"What are the chances the wound will close?" I asked Dr. Cosmetics.

"There's a good possibility it will close to some degree, but it won't ever close completely," he said. "We can speed the healing by installing a Wound VAC. It's basically a sponge bandage adhered to the wound. There's a tube embedded in the sponge that runs to the vacuum unit. Each time the unit cycles on, the sponge is squeezed and the excess fluids in the wound are evacuated through the tube to the unit."

"Anything that will encourage the wound to close," I said.

"The Wound VAC is installed under anesthesia, so we'll schedule you for the OR tomorrow morning."

Christine caught my eye. Another trip to the OR! "You must

have a strong ticker, Jane, for the number of times you've been under," she commented.

§☙   ☙§

The Wound VAC was added to all the paraphernalia I had to drag with me each time I got out of bed. Unplug the Wound VAC from the wall and carry the suitcase-size unit in one hand; in the other hand, guide the IV pole, complete with tubes, bags, and morphine drip dispenser. Don't wait too long to decide you have to get up, or the consequences could be more trouble than leading the parade of equipment.

West Virginia Nancy relieved Christine Saturday evening, and we turned the page to start another week. The Wound VAC performed like a champ, and I visualized all the nasty waste being sucked out of the sponge and dumped into the unit's carafe. Each slurping suck of the tube slowly brought the boundaries of the wound inward.

Monday afternoon, forty-eight hours after installation, Dr. Cosmetics came to remove the sponge. I asked if he'd wait until the next eight-minute interval so I could press the plunger for the next morphine dose. I had no idea what the removal of the sponge would entail, but I didn't want to take any chances.

"I'm going to remove the sponge slowly," he said. "Sometimes the adhesive used to apply it will cause pulling. Let's see how it goes."

"Okay. I'm ready." I closed my eyes and started deep breathing, determined not to interrupt the process. The ripping pain was intolerable. I kept up the deep breathing, gritting my teeth through the rupturing tears, and Dr. Cosmetics kept pulling.

"Can't she have more pain medication?" the attending nurse asked.

Dr. Cosmetics nodded. "Yes, we'll take a break and get you an additional 2 milligrams of morphine."

The nurse ran from the room to get the morphine and was back faster than expected, considering the time needed to requisition and sign out the narcotic. She injected the morphine directly into the IV line, and I felt the drug wash over me. I thanked her in an exhausted whisper, looked toward Dr. Cosmetics, and said, "Okay, I can continue now."

Millimeter by millimeter, the sponge was peeled away from the muscle, leaving black, spongy pebbles embedded in the wound.

West Virginia Nancy stood at the foot of the bed during the whole ordeal, gripping the footboard and quietly praying for my release from the pain.

"Well, it's clear we can't continue with the Wound VAC," Dr. Cosmetics said. "We'll change to wet-to-dry dressings. Or you could have a skin graft to cover the wound. If you want the skin graft, I can do that on Wednesday."

My head was spinning—too much too fast. I couldn't make a quick decision. The thought of another trip to the OR exhausted me. I told him I'd think about it and let him know the next day. I had enough morphine on board at that point that making a clear decision was out of the question.

"Could I have a tissue?" Tears pooled in my eyes and silently cascaded down my cheeks. I took a final deep breath to celebrate the end of the war with the sponge.

"No one should have to go through what you just did, Jane." West Virginia Nancy's tone was serious, controlled, and I think laced with a little anger at Dr. Cosmetics.

The curtain behind my bed parted and there was Ed.

"You just missed it," I said. "Dr. Cosmetics removed the Wound VAC, and it wasn't pretty, but it's over."

He clasped my hand in his, the strength of the squeeze a hint that he had waited nearby so as not to interrupt the procedure and to spare me any indignities. He told me he had decided that having a close female friend help me through the removal process would preserve my dignity in an already emotional and pain-filled situation.

The sparring match with the Wound VAC was over and my

body sagged in relief, burrowing further down into the crinkly hospital mattress and letting the morphine take over and swoop me into sleep. Ed and West Virginia Nancy slipped out of the room and found a quiet corner in the coffee shop to catch their collective breath. Ed told me that they'd chatted about my grueling rounds with surgery and that damn VAC, then without warning, his taking a break turned into his breakdown. He said he'd sobbed without restraint, his face buried in his hands. The façade of strength he'd kept up for me cracked and fell away. He'd been so afraid at the thought of the infection nearly taking me that he'd blubbered like a baby. West Virginia Nancy listened, letting Ed take all the time he'd needed to pour out his sorrow and frustration, and then calmly assured him that things would be better with time.

I drifted off to sleep that night aware that Ed was sitting in the recliner at the foot of my bed. There was no scolding from the nurses that visiting hours were over, just a whispered, "Hi, how are you?" when they came into the room.

The next day, Ed told me that when he'd left for the night, he'd taken the same elevator as the nurse who'd advocated for more morphine during the removal of the Wound VAC.

"She was standing in the back of the elevator car as I stepped on," he said. "She kept her eyes down, and I could see she was upset. She told me that they don't often get cancer patients on this floor and your streak of bad luck was upsetting to her. Then she apologized for showing any upset. She was trained to keep an emotional distance with the patients. I thanked her for her compassion," Ed told me, "and let her know how much we appreciated her care."

❦

In the days that followed, Dr. Cosmetics changed the wet-to-dry bandage by soaking it with saline and then gently pulling it away from the wound. I waited for the eight-minute interval before he began so I could press the blessed plunger for another dose of morphine. I chose not to have the skin graft, even though I wondered if taking the graft from my thigh would result in less cellulite and one thin thigh.

West Virginia Nancy and I filled the days watching Laurel and Hardy films and having quiet chats about our respective dreams. Hers was writing a book for college professors that mirrored Covey's 1990 bestseller, *The 7 Habits of Highly Effective People*. Mine was writing a memoir. I had dabbled in the idea a few years earlier, but the older I got, the more I understood how much the writing of my memoir—the detailed history of my life—was illuminating the present. While West Virginia Nancy and I talked, though, I entertained her with a few of my all-girl-Catholic-school stories, as examples of what I was planning to put in my book.

"Why not write *this* story, Jane?" she eventually asked me. "The story of your journey with breast cancer?"

"No way," I said emphatically. "I'm too close to this forest—no distance to sort out what might help someone else in the same situation. No one wants to read one woman's chronicle isolated from their world."

"Maybe now is not the time. But you should think about it."

§๑　๑§

Kate arrived late Wednesday night to relieve West Virginia Nancy. The GPS in the rental car took her on a back-road route through the streets of the city, ending at the hospital just after nine o'clock. Ed and I were winding down for the night, my energy fading in the late-evening hours, when Kate made a Loretta Young entrance into the room.

"I told the nurses, 'I'm here to see my sister, and if you don't know who I'm talking about, she looks just like me.' Then I flew down the hall. They were fine with me getting here late. I have the fixin's for turkey sammies," she said in a single breath. She was armed with soft rolls, turkey, and swiss cheese.

"Only you, Kate," I said. "Those poor nurses don't know what hit them."

We feasted on the late-night snack, and Ed and I brought Kate up to date on the situation. The following day she would meet all the players. Dr. Cosmetics would be in to change the dressing, and Dr. Infectious Diseases would be in to check the healing progress of the wound.

Kate arrived at the hospital the next day after Dr. Cosmetics had changed the dressing over the wound.

"Kate, I'm being discharged today. Dr. Cosmetics signed the paperwork, and now I have to wait for Dr. Infectious Diseases. I need to be discharged by him, too."

"That's fine. We'll just hang out until he makes his rounds. No sense in hurrying."

It was late afternoon by the time Dr. Infectious Diseases appeared.

"Waiting for me?" he asked as he threw back the curtain.

"Yes," I said, "I need your imprimatur."

I was sitting in the reclining chair, and he leaned over to take a look at the wound. His body blocked Kate's view. He gave me a prescription and instructions to see him in his office next week. The floor nurse discharged me with additional prescriptions from Dr. Cosmetics and detailed instructions on keeping the wound clean.

§🐿 🐿§

Once I was settled in at home, I asked Kate if she wanted to see my wound.

"Sure," she said and eased back against the high dresser in the corner of the bedroom.

When she saw the wound, her mouth dropped open and her eyes locked with Ed's. She kept repeating, "You have got to be kidding!"

I didn't know how to help her absorb the blow. I could see she was emotionally braced to avoid showing any horror that would provoke sadness in me. But a strength I didn't know I had kept me calm.

I asked Ed to take pictures of the wound and of my left breast to show the comparative wreckage. Kate asked what could be done, and I said that Dr. Cosmetics had suggested a skin graft. The wound would close somewhat, he'd said, but never completely. The graft would protect the chest muscle from exposure to bacteria. I'm not sure if that answered her question, but Kate's mind works like a speeding bullet, and she may well have been fast-forwarding to possible legal recourse. Now was not the time to broach that subject, however.

I continued to struggle with changing the dressing, drenching the bandage with saline and then pulling it away from the wound in the smallest of increments. There was one stubborn spot on the wound that would always refuse to let go. I stood in the shower until the saturated dressing began to slide off, hanging only by that spot until I slowly edged the last bit away, gritting my teeth in anticipation of the ripping and tearing.

After two weeks of this, I was at my lowest. My body bent forward at the waist from the abdominal incision and quivered with the tension of a taut string.

"How are you doing in there, Jane?" Ed called from the bedroom.

"Not very well," I whispered, trying in vain to choke back my tears. I'd just stepped out of the shower.

"Please let me help you. I want to be there to help you," he pleaded.

Like a little baby unable to do for herself, I acquiesced. He threw a big bath towel over my shoulders and gently patted me dry. The mirror reflected a bent-over old lady crushed under the weight of sorrow.

∾   ∾

A wound culture taken the day before I was discharged showed no signs of further infection, and Dr. Infectious Diseases convinced me that the wound would never close measurably. While the area was clean, he suggested, I should cover everything up with a skin graft. That would be the procedure that would finally bring this nightmare to an end. I fought against the idea of covering up the damage and concealing the evidence, but I agreed to the graft, knowing I had the pictures of the open wound. Subconsciously, I wanted someone to answer for this debacle.

I remembered that when I was wheeled into surgery for the removal of the TRAM flap, one of the operating room nurses had said, "We tried to keep everything as sterile as we could." That was an unsolicited comment that I'd stashed away in my mind, where I was keeping a running record of discovery.

Christine returned to be with me for the skin graft. She'd been with me for the first surgery, the lumpectomy, and now the last. A thin four-by-six-inch slice of my right thigh was removed and run through some sort of tenderizer to make the skin thin and stretchy before being applied to the chest wound. I was gratified to know that the days of changing the dressing were over. Of course, the days of hope for reconstruction were over, too.

The skin graft was an outpatient procedure that didn't take long. It was scheduled for the morning, and we were in the car and headed home by early afternoon. "If I never see this hospital again, it'll be too soon," I said.

"I know," said Christine. "I know."

Chapter Sixteen

Denouement—Not Every Memory Is Soaked in Sorrow

The ghost of my right breast was a thin, white waffle of grafted skin. Any thoughts of future reconstruction were set aside since the skin graft didn't have the elasticity required to insert an expander. Leaving well enough alone was my best option. I was relieved beyond belief that the pain from the wound simply disappeared with the application of the graft. I set about getting my life back to the normal I'd known. All along this journey, as each treatment or surgery took some part of me away, I'd face the initial jolt and resign myself to assimilating the changes in my body. These outward changes were what they were, and, in time, the visible scars would heal. Changes to my psyche were another matter. I struggled to keep my optimism afloat and stubbornly believed I could heal the inner scars with diet and exercise.

My conviction that all was well and back on track was set aright by my new family doctor. On the advice of my surgeon, I began looking for an internist. After I called two or three and found that they were not taking new patients, Ed suggested that I call his doctor, with whom he'd been treating for over twenty years. Doc Bee agreed to take me as a new patient on the strength of my relationship with Ed. My first appointment was an informal chat so that he could get to know me face-to-face rather than through all the reports forwarded to him from the surgeons, the oncologist, and the radiologist. I had a thick paper file but thin skin. All Doc Bee had to ask was, "How did you meet Ed?" and the waterworks started.

I'd been harboring so much pent-up fear from fighting an indefatigable foe that the very mention of Ed's name tipped the scales. I told Doc Bee about meeting Ed in karate class and being impressed by his kindness toward a beginner. There he'd been, all decked out in black belt and stripes, and I couldn't even tie the belt. Instead of a gruff reply, he'd motioned to a nearby student to help me out. I told Doc Bee how, years later, I'd run into Ed again getting coffee at a convenience store—a chance meeting that grew into a partnership.

"I don't mind tears," Doc Bee said.

"That's good," I sobbed. "How do you feel about deep breathing?" I pulled myself together and answered his next question.

"Is there anything I should be paying attention to today?" I knew this question was pro forma, my opening to steer the conversation. I took the chance to get his opinion about the increasing feeling I'd been having that I was losing my emotional grip.

"Well," I began, "I seem to be going through periods of real sadness, and not just the regular mood swings. This is extreme. I cry without provocation, I feel trapped inside myself, and I can't separate mood from madness."

"When you have these bouts, how do you feel?" he asked.

"Imprisoned … separated. I'm immobilized when the funk flies in. I've tried to get a grip on things with diet and exercise."

Doc Bee patted my arm and wheeled his chair back against a table. He shook his head and assured me that I wasn't the first one to describe symptoms of depression and still think that diet and exercise would be a cure-all.

"This isn't entirely surprising, considering what you've been through," he explained. "You'll always be waiting for the other shoe to drop and looking for stray marks and feeling stray pains that might signal a recurrence of the cancer."

Who, me? Depressed? I don't think so! I can pull it together in the worst of situations. I'd met challenges along the way that had my stomach roiling with anxiety. Like the first time I spoke in public, when my heart pounded so loudly I was certain that those in the front row could hear the beating. Or the time my high school biology teacher accused me of sassing her. My mouth dropped open, my heart raced, and the blood drained from my face as I took in the clean, soapy scent of her nun's habit. She was pale with upset, too. All I could do was apologize in a quivery little voice. And then there was the time when my checking account was overdrawn and the owner of a restaurant offered to cash a postdated check. His cashier gave me a look of pure disdain, but I refused to let him make me feel like scum. I walked out with my check and never looked back. Most notably, I had weathered the loss of both my parents. Handling the aftermath of a disease wasn't any different, as far as I could see. Just let me get started; I'd be able to figure out how to bring my emotions under control. But I was wrong.

From the day of my diagnosis, I'd tackled the disease head-on. Searching in books and online, I'd vowed to be informed, to ask questions, to stay in control. Now, the lid of that weight had been lifted—I was at the end of the year from hell. Yet, instead of relief, depression had flown out from under the lid, blindsiding me with a grip too firm to pry loose.

I'd lost interest in my hobbies and my energy had decreased. I tried to engage in a cross-stitch project or a jigsaw puzzle because neither required high-powered thinking or had to be finished in one go. I would find myself stopping midstitch or just holding a puzzle piece in my hand, and I'd be staring out the window, completely disengaged. I'd analyze my technique in making a french knot, or in sorting the puzzle pieces, and compare it to what someone else might think. Would I measure up to someone else's standards for stitching and sorting?

Doc Bee patiently sketched a simplistic continuum of

depression, ranging from anxiety to melancholy, to illustrate the finer points of his diagnosis. I fit on the melancholy end of the continuum. I had highs and lows, just like everyone else did, but mine were all below that imaginary line that defined normalcy. He recommended a low dose of an antidepressant medication that would help correct the extremes in the highs and lows and bring them nearer to that imaginary line.

"Really?" I asked. "I don't see myself as someone who needs an antidepressant. And that drug seems like one of the big guns."

"It's been around for a very long time, and we know a lot about it. If it were necessary, I'd prescribe this drug for my wife," Doc Bee assured me.

I put myself in his hands and accepted my state of mind. With that, my body and my mind were on the mend.

§♌ ♌§

From diagnosis to denouement, my dance with the beast was laced with veins of humor that held firm the weave of the net far below the tight wire of surgeries and treatments. From Marian, the cranial prosthesis fitter at the wig boutique, to Esther, the breast prosthesis fitter who insisted I was a D cup, there were a lot of amazing people who added a little comic relief to an experience that was unspeakably scary.

Whether somber or absurd, each phase of the journey was punctuated with the support of my family and my friends. The rekindling of sibling relationships was initially tentative, as my sisters and brothers and I scrambled to understand our respective roles in this unscripted drama. We had nothing to fall back on in our childhood experiences that came close to knowing how to cope with watching a loved one dwindle away.

Despite my being an a la carte Catholic, a fallen angel so to speak, there's no denying the effect of the basic mantras of my childhood on the way I negotiated the labyrinth of medicine and madness. The nuns taught me to take tough times on the chin, that whatever happened was God's will. Mom always said, "Rise to the occasion," or, "Offer it up for the poor souls in purgatory." And Daddy always said, "Mind your mother." Consequently, an acceptance of God's will, as well as grit and obedience, was the basis of my character when the beast tapped me on the shoulder and asked, "Shall we dance?"

The invitation to dance was an invitation to join an elite club. One membership requirement was to face my mortality—to look death in the eye and decide how I felt about wrapping up the loose ends of earthly ties. I reconciled myself to that possible outcome very early in the journey. I had to so that I could be freed up to concentrate on coping with what would be asked of me to regain my health.

Before this happened, I would often tease about having my story ready for St. Peter when I reach the pearly gates. My opening line was going to be, "Before you say anything, St. Peter, let me explain." But now I'd like to hope that this fight with cancer has cancelled out some of the demerits on my permanent record.

I am a survivor, but I didn't come out of the fight unscathed. You've read about the wracking of the flesh. I hinted at the struggle of the mind. You know I chased illusions of success as defined by others. In the end, I have put away the frustration of having no recourse to reconstruction. I have separated mood from madness. I have stopped chasing the moving target of illusion and no longer delay chasing my dreams. Delaying dreams stifles hope.

> Hope is a thing with feathers
> That perches in the soul
> And sings the tune
> Without the words
> And never stops at all.
> —Emily Dickinson

Afterword

That was then and this is now.

Ed and I celebrated our sixth anniversary in 2009. He lives in his boyhood home, and I live with my three cats in a townhouse about one mile away. My illness was a test to our commitment at a very early stage of the relationship. No matter how many times I suggested to Ed that he bow out gracefully before things got too bad, he'd look at me with solemn eyes and say, "You're going to have to do better than this to get rid of me."

After my diagnosis, my family was much more than a photograph of eleven siblings that I'd show to Ed while offering short anecdotes to help him remember who was who. Each one became three-dimensional through their gestures of kindness and sacrifice. I put a china plate—an orphaned Wedgwood I'd found in the dishwasher of an apartment I'd rented—on the living room table that holds the family picture, to put all the cards from family and friends. The pile grew over the months and beckoned all visitors to sit and read. There are no sweeter words to someone who is sick than those of support and encouragement.

§℞   ℞§

My best friend, Virginia Jan, passed away in August 2005 after an eighteen-month battle with cancer. She was a class act and the quintessence of an informed patient, arming herself with information and questions before each appointment with a doc.

They were kept on their toes and held to a standard that demanded she be viewed as an intelligent woman, savvy consumer of medical care, and someone who would be involved in the decisions all along the way. Over twenty-seven years of friendship, we'd shared the highs and lows of each other's lives, never dreaming we'd share a journey that begins with a diagnosis of cancer and extends across time in a series of battles to survive. I delivered Virginia Jan's eulogy in September 2005, to a standing-room-only gathering of her friends, family, and colleagues.

§∞   ∞§

I wrestled with whether or not to pursue legal action with regard to the breast reconstruction disaster. My sisters were in support of my doing just that. Their encouragement ranged from, "Jane, find the most expensive lawyer you can," to "Think about it, Jane. A half-million dollars would make a nice early retirement."

I was so exhausted from fighting the fight of the disease, I couldn't imagine having the energy to go through what would surely be a long and drawn-out legal process. Could I sit across a table from Dr. Cosmetics and accuse him of malpractice? What about the nurse in the OR the night the TRAM was removed? And, of course, there was also the nurse who, during my recovery from the reconstruction surgery, astutely observed that the site shouldn't feel cold to the touch. Would she give testimony?

No regrets. My decision was the best for me at the time. Retribution was not mine to exact. As my mom used to quote from Longfellow: "Though the mills of God grind slowly, yet they grind exceeding small; Though with patience He stands waiting, with exactness grinds He all."

§∞   ∞§

My application for promotion was denied two years running.

With each unsuccessful application, I carefully scrutinized my dossier looking for ways to improve the presentation of my work. I spoke with a member of the evaluation committee but came away dissatisfied with the vague and general responses to my direct questions about why my work was ranked too low to be considered for promotion by the administration. I walked away from that meeting determined to take my future into my own hands and relinquish the false hopes of illusion. The weight that was lifted off my shoulders with that decision was nearly tangible. I marked the occasion by buying a pressboard cupboard at Target and stashing away all of my documents on its shelves. The cupboard is in the basement, and I don't even see it when I walk past. Quixotic windmills no longer lure me.

I'm beginning my sixteenth year at the same university. I never entertained the option of denying myself the elixir of teaching because of my disappointment in the system. I revel in my students' successes and enjoy the rigor of challenging their thinking about how to teach reading. All of my students are studying to be elementary school teachers. The majority of them aspire to teaching the primary grades: first, second, or third. Over the course of the semester, their eyes are opened to the complexities of teaching literacy to the point where each one who aspires to the hardest job in the school, teaching a child to read, must resolve anew to meet that challenge.

§๑   ๑₹

I am five years cancer free. The beast was dealt a blow that keeps me optimistic about my long-term survival. However, the many surgeries, chemo, and radiation have left a few reminders that I carry with me every day.

One such reminder is moderate lymphedema in my right arm. Picture the lymph system as a necklace of little pearls that runs below the skin, carrying immune cells in its fluid and distributing them throughout the body. Since a large number of my lymph nodes were removed at the time of the lumpectomy, there's a snag in my necklace of pearls that causes fluid retention and tissue swelling. I manage my lymphedema by wearing a compression sleeve and gauntlet during the day, which allows my arm to stand up to additional activities, such as carrying books to and from classes. At the end of the day, I set aside thirty minutes to massage my arm using techniques that I learned from my lymphedema therapist, and then I wrap my arm with compression bandages for the night. These thirty minutes have become a respite of peace.

A second reminder is chronic fatigue. Long-term effects from the radiation and the failed reconstruction still keep a tight hold on my energy. I manage the fatigue by conserving my energy during the academic semesters so that I can be at the top of my game in my teaching. My weekends are reserved for utter relaxation, indulging in activities that feed my soul.

Both my oncologist and my surgeon discharged me in 2009. Being released from this level of medical care was a momentous gesture that said to me, "Jane, you're no longer defined in any measure by your illness. Go sit in front of a mirror and sing, 'I Enjoy Being a Girl.' Then dance in the yard with ribbons in your hair."

Acknowledgments

For their untiring support during my illness and subsequently the writing of this memoir, my sincerest appreciation goes out to my choir of angels: My sisters, Christine and Kate, who literally flew to my aid; and Mary, Celeste, Patti, and Donna Grace, who wished me well and kept in touch with calls, cards, and sparkly treasures. My brothers, Jimmy, Bill, Joe, and Eddie each of whom got misty-eyed at the thought of their sister in trouble. My longtime friends, Milwaukee Carole and West Virginia Nancy who were among the flying angels who interceded on my behalf when I couldn't advocate for myself. My colleagues Donna, Sandy, Kim, and Judy who masterminded coverage of my classes and explained the situation to my students because I just couldn't do it without emotional upset. To Virginia Jan, my longtime friend and fellow cancer patient, I thought of you so often as I wrote this story and still shake my head in disbelief that you are gone. Special thanks to my surgeon, Daleela Dodge, for lending medical credibility to my story in her fabulous foreword. Abounding thanks to Ed, who lived every moment of this journey with me and read every word of this work many times over with inimitable patience and support.

Lightning Source UK Ltd.
Milton Keynes UK
UKOW041051040313

207099UK00001B/239/P